P-38

Lightning

PILOT'S FLIGHT OPERATING INSTRUCTIONS

©2010 Periscope Film LLC
All Rights Reserved
ISBN #978-1-935327-93-6   1-935327-93-3
www.PeriscopeFilm.com

PILOT TRAINING MANUAL FOR THE

Lightning

P·38

PILOT TRAINING MANUAL FOR THE

Lightning

P-38

PUBLISHED FOR HEADQUARTERS, AAF

OFFICE OF ASSISTANT CHIEF OF AIR STAFF, TRAINING

BY HEADQUARTERS, AAF, OFFICE OF FLYING SAFETY

G & P CINCINNATI 12-2-44 10000

Foreword

   This manual is the text for your training as a P-38 pilot.
The Air Forces' most experienced training and supervisory personnel
have collaborated to make it a complete exposition of
what your duties as a pilot are, how each duty will be performed,
and why it must be performed in the manner prescribed.

   The techniques and procedures described in this book are
standard and mandatory. In this respect the manual serves the dual
purpose of a training checklist and a working handbook.
Use it to make sure that you learn everything described herein.
Use it to study and review the essential facts concerning everything
taught. Such additional self-study and review will not only
advance your training, but will alleviate the burden of your already
overburdened instructors.

   This training manual does not replace the Technical Orders for
the airplane, which will always be your primary source of
information concerning the P-38 so long as you fly it. This is essentially
the textbook of the P-38. Used properly, it will enable you to
utilize the pertinent Technical Orders to even greater advantage.

GENERAL, U.S. ARMY
COMMANDING GENERAL
ARMY AIR FORCES

SECTION 1 INTRODUCTION

HISTORY

In the spring of 1937 the United States Army Air Corps submitted to various manufacturers specifications for a high altitude fighter airplane.

To fill these requirements of performance, armament, and adaptability, the Lockheed Aircraft Corporation embarked on the construction of a radically different model, later designated the XP-38.

This highly experimental model was completed and ready for test in December of 1938. Lt. Ben Kelsey, pilot and engineer, was given the dubious honor of testing the new airplane. One night late in December, the XP-38 was dismantled and transported by trucks to March Field. By the middle of January, 1939, Kelsey began the conventional ground tests.

Even then numerous rumors had started concerning the future of the XP-38. Its twin booms and tricycle landing gear certainly deviated from the conventional. These, coupled with two engines and dual engine controls, appeared to be too much for one man to handle, according to the hangar talk. The brakes failed during a fast taxi run, and heads nodded an "I told you so." Undaunted, Kelsey carried on and a few days later was ready for the first takeoff.

Again the hangar boys wagged their heads when the XP started a violent shaking as it became airborne on its first takeoff. Thanks to Kelsey's skill the XP continued to fly—a whole half hour. The ailment was corrected and subsequent test flights were made.

Early in February, the XP left on a cross country flight to Wright Field where a brief check would decide its acceptability. It made the hop from March Field to Wright Field in 5 hours and 33 minutes flying time. Kelsey had a brief conference with General Arnold, and then took off for Mitchel Field, N. Y. Forty-two minutes later the XP made the headlines by cracking up in a creek 200 yards from Mitchel Field.

Discouraged, but not quitting, the manufacturers started the YP-38, the first of 13 for the U.S. Army Air Corps.

The YP, like its predecessor the XP, made the headlines—and in a detrimental fashion. Eventually it became common knowledge, as any Southern California citizen could testify, that the "Yippy" was a jinx airplane.

The pilot was a doomed man if anything went wrong. He could not bail out, the tail had a nasty habit of shaking off, and the plane could not be pulled out of a dive.

The British and French, hard pressed for airplanes, contracted to purchase more than 600 P-38's. They specified certain modifications. They insisted that there be no turbo-superchargers or counter-rotation propellers. As expected, the airplane gave a very poor performance. Again the insults grew. It seemed as if the P-38 was doomed to die a dishonorable death.

A small nucleus of factory and Army men, including Kelsey, never lost faith. The manufacturer continued production with original designs.

Training new pilots for the airplane was slow. It was a lot of airplane to step into and take up alone. All was not lost, however. The manufacturer came to the rescue, and, with the sanction of General Giles, Jimmie Mattern introduced the "Piggyback" as a training aid. The Piggyback, probably one of the greatest single training aids, tremendously increased the efficiency of the training program. It did much to dispel numerous baseless rumors about the P-38.

The tempo of training and producing fighter pilots for the airplane kept increasing. Yet the crucial test of meeting and bettering the enemy had yet to come.

First contact with the enemy was made in the Aleutians, August 4, 1942. Two P-38's met and shot down three type 97 Japanese flying boats. Ten days later, over Iceland, a P-38 shot down a Focke-Wolf Kurier. The christening had occurred. The skeptics claimed this proved nothing. Several weeks later over France, the Lightnings were unable to make contact with the enemy, and again the skeptics had a chance to gloat.

Fate finally relented, and in November 1942 the P-38 received its real test in the North African invasion. Taking the Luftwaffe on under all conditions, the black sheep became a white hope—the queen of the African skies. The same excellent reports poured in from the Aleutians, and the Southwest Pacific. It was in the Southwest Pacific that 12 P-38's without loss to themselves disposed of 15 Zeros. Said one bewildered Jap pilot: "Two airplanes—one pilot!"

The P-38 had won its spurs. It became the darling of the bomber boys for bringing them home. New fields were tried—all with the same success. Dive-bombing, skip-bombing, and strafing became part of the day's work for "The Forked Devil," as the men of the Luftwaffe called the Lightning.

The P-38 not only dishes it out; it can take it:

A few recorded cases: Captain Hoelle clipped a telephone pole while strafing. His ship was horribly battered, but he came back.

One lad lost an engine 5 times over Kiska but made it home each time.

A P-38 pilot left 3 feet of wing on a Jap destroyer and brought his plane back.

Jack Illfrey flew home on one engine with 2 holes in the good propeller and 168 holes in his airplane.

Here's how Lt. Ben Kelsey describes the P-38: "This comfortable old cluck will fly like hell, fight like a wasp upstairs, and land like a butterfly." He adds: "As a fighting ship it's just like a big girl and you have to take her up on your lap and manhandle her. It's an extremely honest airplane; it doesn't bite and doesn't do unexpected things."

COMBAT EXPERIENCE

The reputation of a fighter airplane depends on the destruction it deals out to the enemy, the protection it gives the pilot, and the way the men who fly it feel about it. They must be convinced that their plane is the best in the world.

The P-38 is a leading fighter of World War II. It has a very long range, enabling it to give bomber support deep into enemy territory. It fights equally well at high or low altitudes. The P-38 is also a fighter bomber, capable of carrying 2 tons of bombs.

Its four .50-cal. machine guns and one 20-mm. cannon, all mounted in the nose, produce a concentration of fire power ideal for strafing. The safety factor of 2 engines has endeared it to fighter pilots who call the second engine their "round trip ticket." With one engine knocked out, P-38 pilots in combat have finished the fight and made it home.

The P-38 has demonstrated a remarkable adaptability. It has met the enemy on all fronts, coping equally well with the changing needs of different situations.

High altitude fighter

Two turbo-superchargers give the Allison engines sea level horsepower at extremely high altitudes. The success of the P-38 as a high altitude escort in the European theatre and as a high altitude intercepter in the Southwest Pacific area has established an enviable combat record.

Low altitude fighter and fighter-bomber

Sweeping in at mast height, P-38's have sunk many German, Italian, and Japanese ships. The presence of all the guns in the nose, rather than the wings, eliminates criss-crossing cones of fire. It has an effective straight-ahead range of more than 600 yards, making it excellent for strafing.

A flight of P-38's can go into action with all guns blazing while at the same time carrying a bomb load capable of sinking the largest vessels. The P-38 has won fame as a dive bomber and skip bomber in every theatre of war in addition to its other successes.

Escort fighter

Carrying droppable fuel tanks, the P-38 has a range of more than 1000 miles. It was the first fighter to fly the Atlantic and can be ferried to any fighting front. It was also the first fighter to go all the way with bombers on long range missions.

Photo-reconnaissance

The photo-reconnaissance version of the Lightning is known as the F-5. Instead of the usual 4 machine guns and 1 cannon, the F-5 has 5 cameras. Its pilot can take pictures straight down and obliquely.

Pilots who fly F-5's come in sometimes at tree-top height, take their pictures, and are gone before enemy anti-aircraft guns can be trained on them. Or again, they come over at 30,000 feet and take pictures so clear that you can pick out automobile tire tracks in the enlarged prints. Unarmed, and generally alone, these F-5's, because of their great range and tremendous speed, are among the finest photo-reconnaissance ships in the world.

"Boy! That's a lot of Airplane"

GENERAL DESCRIPTION

"Boy, that's a lot of airplane!"

The P-38 is a big fighter plane. It stands almost 10 feet high, spreads out 52 feet, and is over 37½ feet long.

When the impression of size ceases to be a novelty, you notice some rather peculiar looking features. The long slender booms tapering into twin rudders are unique in aircraft design.

A closer inspection from the front quarter shows that the P-38 is a midwing airplane, with 2 liquid-cooled engines and 2 three-bladed propellers. It has a streamlined center section, called a gondola, and stands solidly on a tricycle landing gear. There are four .50-cal. machine guns and one 20-mm. cannon in the nose.

Right under the wing between the engines and the gondola, you can see two odd projections. They are shackles for external tanks or bombs. The plane can carry quite a payload on these shackles.

As you turn around to the right of the airplane, the slender profile comes into view. The

8

clean lines of the boom are broken in 3 places. On the forward portion of the boom, right under the wing, is a large tear-shaped ram air intake. Just behind the wing and on top of the boom is the turbo-supercharger. In the center of the boom is the prominent coolant radiator and shutter.

Continuing around to the rear, you see the horizontal stabilizer and the elevator with its

counterweights for dynamic stability. Looking over the tail section, you have a good rear view of the plexiglas enclosure of the cockpit.

The P-38 is a most impressive looking airplane. You wonder if you can handle it, but you needn't worry. With a little time and application on your part, and whether you fire guns or cameras, the P-38 will become a formidable weapon in your hands.

INSTRUCTION PRIOR TO FIRST FLIGHT

Study and understand all the Technical Orders pertaining to the P-38. Every P-38 series is different. An experienced pilot of a P-38G must have the proper cockpit time before he flies a P-38L or any other series. There are many modifications, relocations of controls, and differences in operation that he must know.

Read your Pilots' Information File, AAF Flying Regulations, and your Base Flying Regulations.

Cockpit Explanation

Your Flight Leader will give you a complete cockpit explanation. The explanation will include the location and operation of all instruments, switches, and controls.

COCKPIT TIME

Cockpit time is your introduction to the P-38. Take advantage of it. Rehearse procedures. Read and re-read the checklists.

You will spend a minimum of 5 hours in the cockpit of the P-38 series you are going to fly. Study all the instruments and cockpit installations. Become so well acquainted with every instrument and control that you are at home in the cockpit on your first solo flight and are prepared for any emergency.

The necessity for developing a thorough cockpit routine cannot be overemphasized. Hit-and-miss skipping about the cockpit results in forgetting some essential check. **Always check the cockpit from left to right.** Use the checklist.

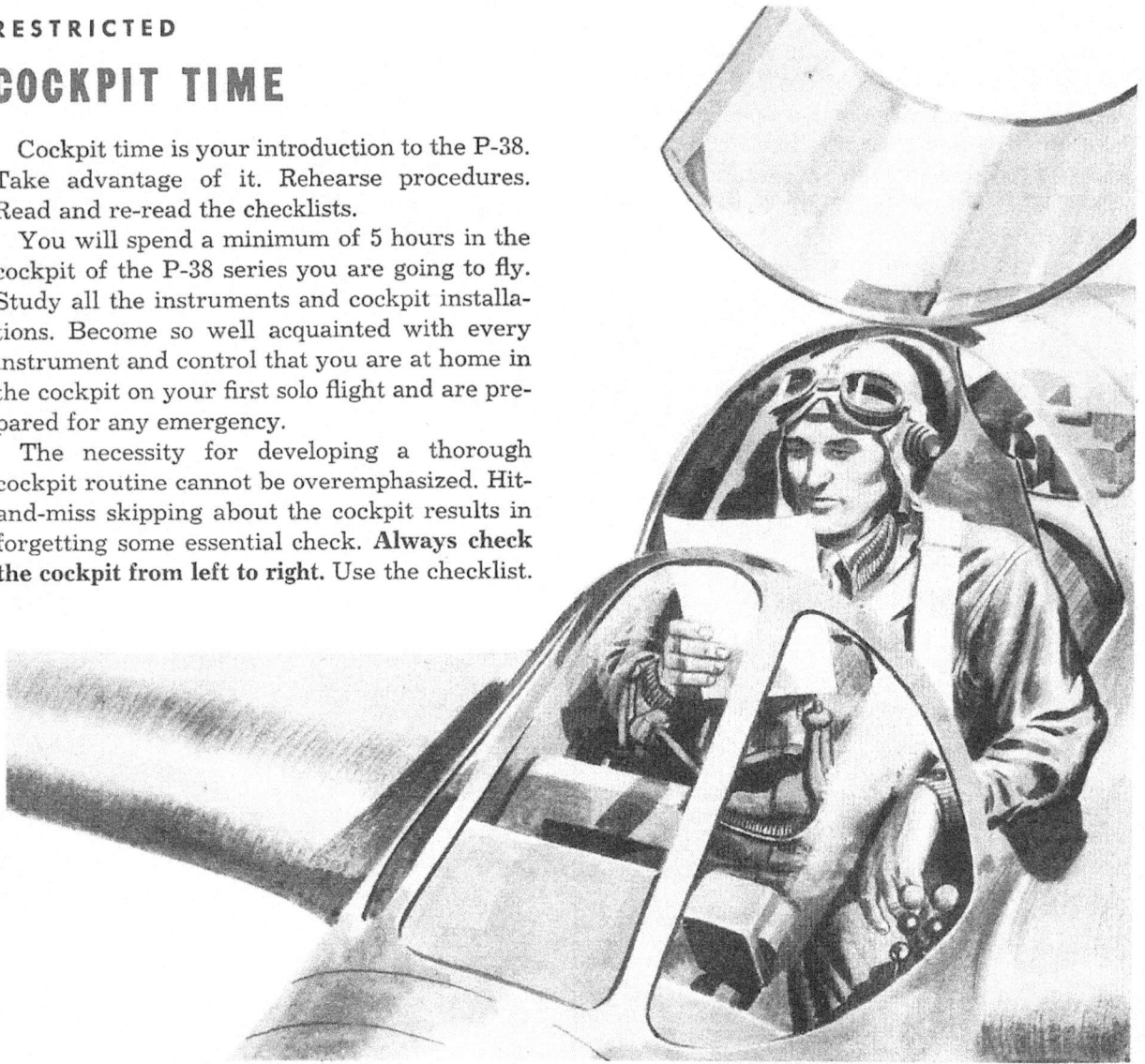

BLINDFOLD TEST

You are required to pass a blindfold test. Blindfolded, you have to locate and operate all instruments, switches, and controls. This is when well spent cockpit time pays dividends.

Make a cockpit check before starting, after starting, before takeoff, in flight, before landing, and after cutting the engines.

PIGGYBACK DEMONSTRATION

After five hours' cockpit time, you receive a demonstration flight in a piggyback P-38. Make every minute of this ride count. Know what the instructor is doing from the time you both enter the cockpit until the flight is over and the engines are cut off.

The first thing you do after you and the pilot are in the piggyback, is get out again. Rehearse the recommended piggyback bailout procedure. You know then, before you take off, how you leave the airplane if during the flight you have to bail out. Wear a back pack B-8 type parachute which gives you more movement. You leave first and the pilot follows. If you are too large to leave while the pilot is in the cockpit, you hold the control wheel as the pilot leaves and then go out after him.

The Demonstration and What to Look For

Power-on stall—gear and flaps up. Power-off stall—gear and flaps down. Look for airspeed and attitude.

Accelerated stalls. Look for airspeed and buffet.

Tight turns—with and without flaps. Look for degree of turn and maneuverability.

ACROBATICS

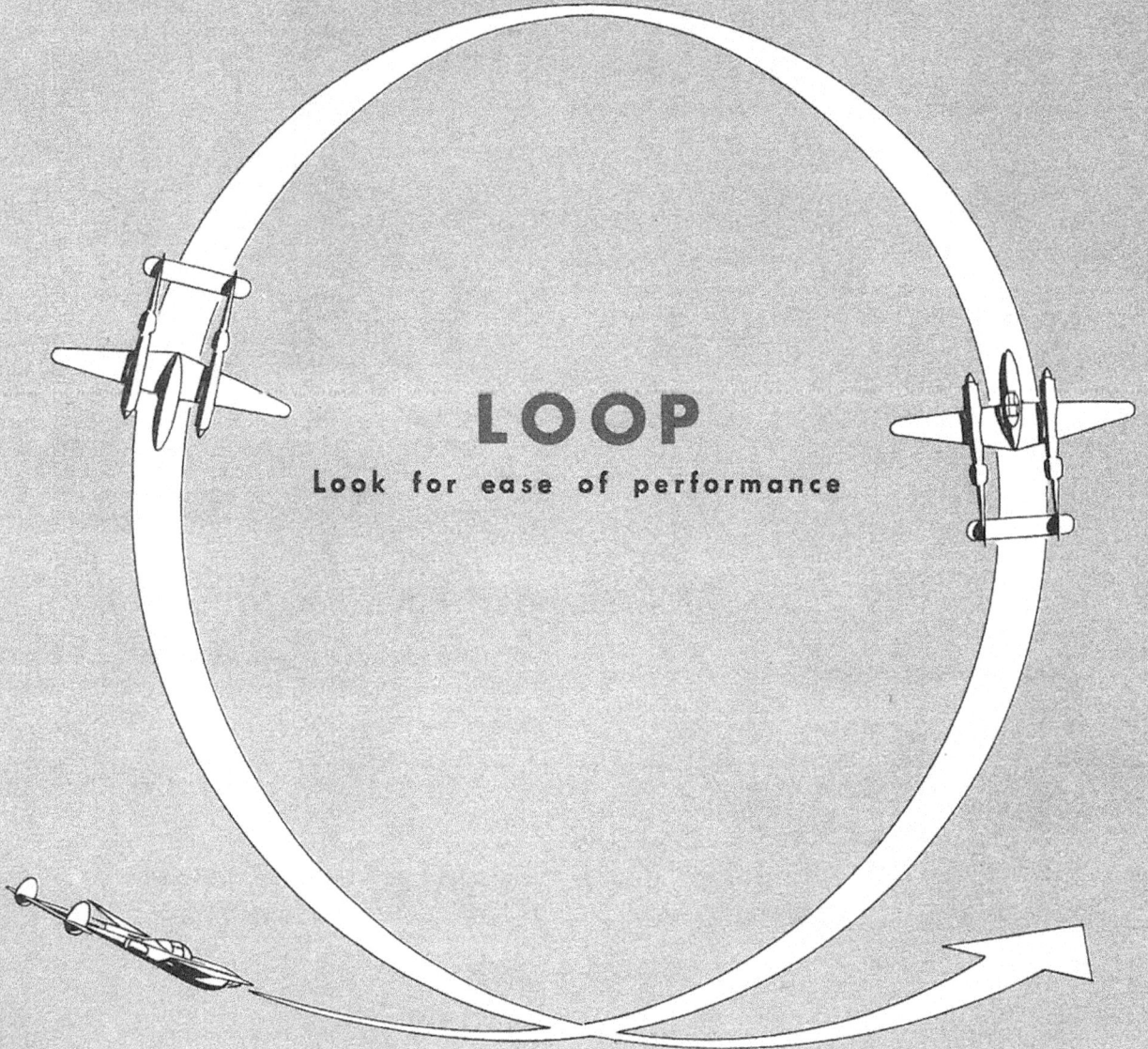

LOOP
Look for ease of performance

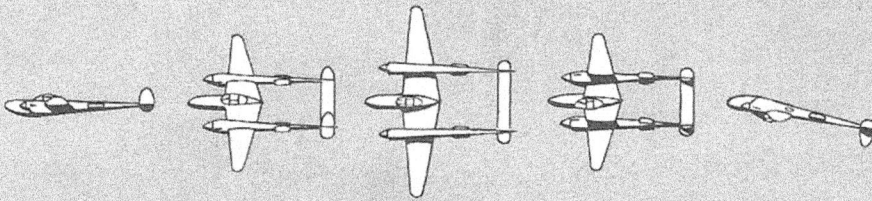

IMMELMANN

Look for maneuverability

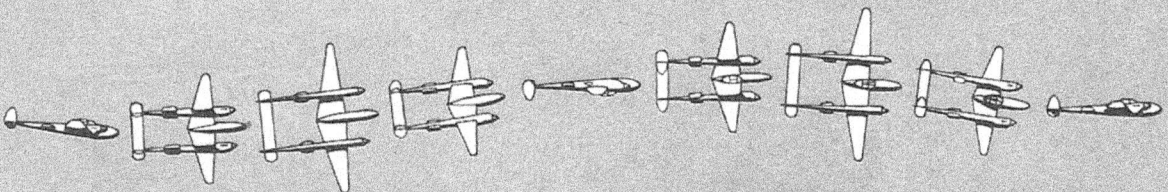

SLOW ROLL

Look for accuracy and technique

NOTE: This maneuver is always done to the left. A slow roll to the right can cause the nosewheel door to pop open and break off.

The Demonstration and What to Look For

At 5000 feet, simulated engine failure on takeoff. Note altitude doesn't go below 5000 feet.

Look for simulated takeoff conditions:
Gear down.
90 mph IAS.
Takeoff manifold pressure and rpm.
Retract landing gear.
Accelerate to 120 mph.

Close throttle. Simulated engine failure.

Maintain directional control. Look for procedure:
Close mixture control.
Feather propeller.
Trim.

Note: This demonstration will be done with booster pumps OFF. Fuel selector and ignition **are not** to be turned OFF.

14

The Demonstration and What to Look For

•

Single engine dive at 300 mph IAS. Notice rudder pressure diminishes with acceleration.

•

Single engine turns to right and left; shallow and steep. Look for single engine performance.

•

Unfeathering propeller. Look for procedure.

•

Normal approach and landing. Look for pattern, altitude, and airspeeds.

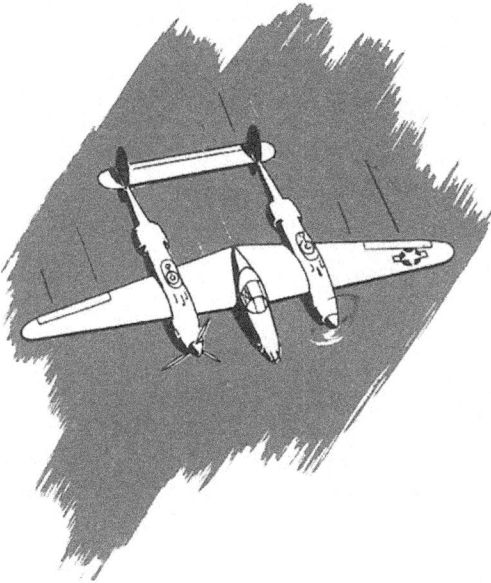

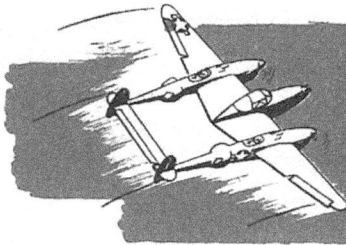

SECTION 2 EQUIPMENT

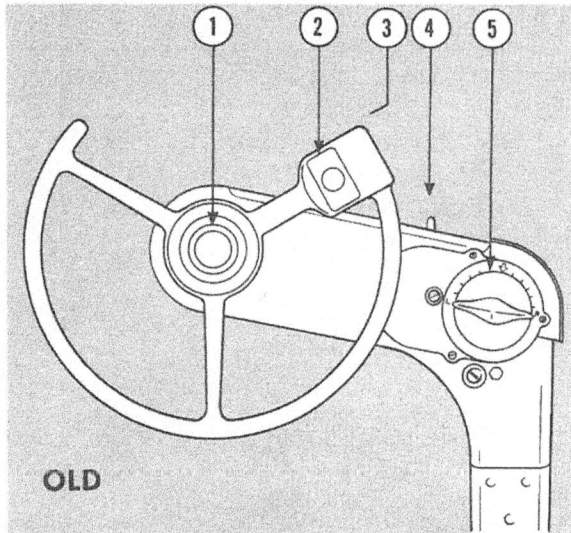

OLD

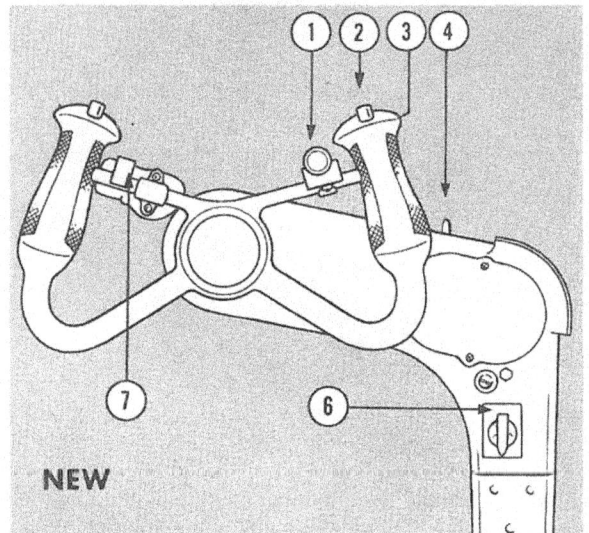

NEW

CONTROL WHEEL

1. Radio transmitter button.
2. Cannon button.
3. Machine gun button (back of wheel).
4. Gun selector switch box.
5. Aileron trim tab control. P-38's with aileron boost do not have an aileron trim tab control.
6. Gun sight light rheostat.
7. Dive flap control.

SURFACE CONTROL LOCK

Lock the flight controls by the tube assembly on the right-hand window sill.

To set the lock:

1. Put rudders in neutral.
2. Push the right end of the locking tube forward of the guiding angle.
3. Place the left end of the tube in the clip on the left window sill.
4. Strap the tube to the center of the control wheel.

On the P-38L and later P-38J's the surface control lock does not lock the rudders.

Before takeoff, check the controls for freedom of movement and be sure the control lock is stowed in place.

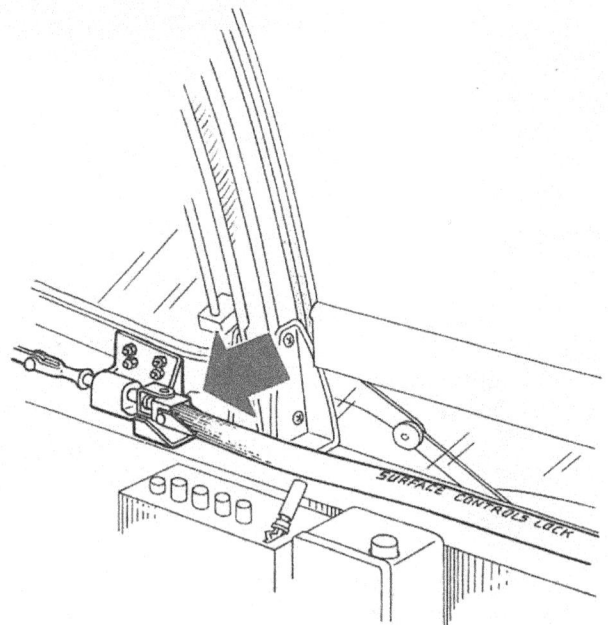

COCKPIT—LEFT-HAND SIDE

1. Spotlight (normal position).
2. Throttles.
3. Surface controls lock clip.
4. Propeller controls.
5. Propeller selector switches.
6. Mixture controls.
7. Propeller warning lights (P-38H only).
8. Carburetor air filter control. (Late airplanes.)
9. Propeller circuit breaker buttons.
10. Gun charger handle (on early airplanes only).
11. Ignition switches.
12. Cannon trigger button. (Machine gun button on forward side of wheel.)
13. Propeller feathering switches.
14. Parking brake handle.
15. Microphone button. (Location varies with airplane model.)
16. Gun charging selector-knob. (Early airplanes only.)
17. Landing gear warning light. (Early airplanes only.)
18. Propeller lever vernier knob.
19. Friction control.
20. Bomb or tank release selector switches.
21. Bomb or tank release indicator lights.
22. Cockpit light.
23. Gun (or camera) compartment heat control. (Cockpit heat on later airplanes.)
24. Arm-safe switch. (Bombs.)
25. Arming indicator light.
26. Safe indicator light.
27. Bomb or droppable tank release button.
28. Spare indicator lights.
29. Spotlight alternate position socket.
30. Cockpit ventilator control.
31. Gun sight dark glass stowage. (Early airplanes only.)
32. Landing gear control handle.
33. Landing gear control release.
34. Oxygen pressure gage.
35. Elevator tab control.
36. Engine primer.

TYPICAL INSTRUMENT PANEL

P-38J-25 Panel Shown

1. Standby magnetic compass.
2. Suction gage.
3. Clock.
4. Gyro horizon.
5. Manifold pressure gages (left and right).
6. Tachometers (left and right).
7. Engine gage right engine (oil temperature and pressure and fuel pressure).
8. Coolant temperature gage.
9. Carburetor air temperature gage.
10. BC-608 contactor.
11. Generator switches.
12. Ammeters.
13. Compass correction cards.
14. Engine gage left engine (oil temperature and pressure and fuel pressure).
15. Rate of climb indicator.
16. Bank and turn indicator.
17. Airspeed indicator.
18. Directional gyro.
19. Remote indicating compass.
20. Front (reserve) fuel tanks quantity gage.
21. Rear (main) fuel tanks quantity gage.
22. Hydraulic pressure gage.
23. Altimeter.
24. Landing gear warning light.
25. Landing gear warning light test button.
26. Spare bulb.

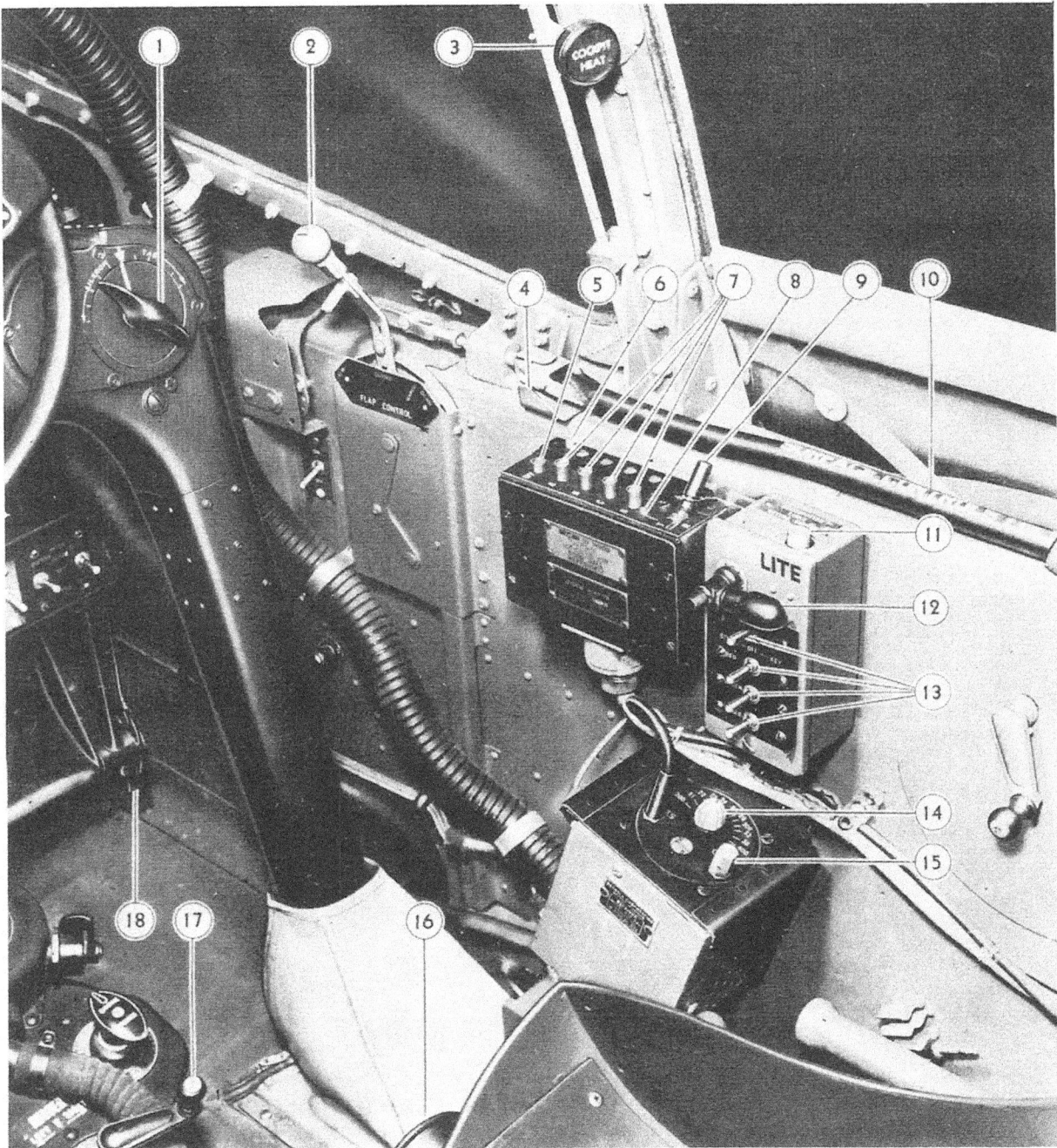

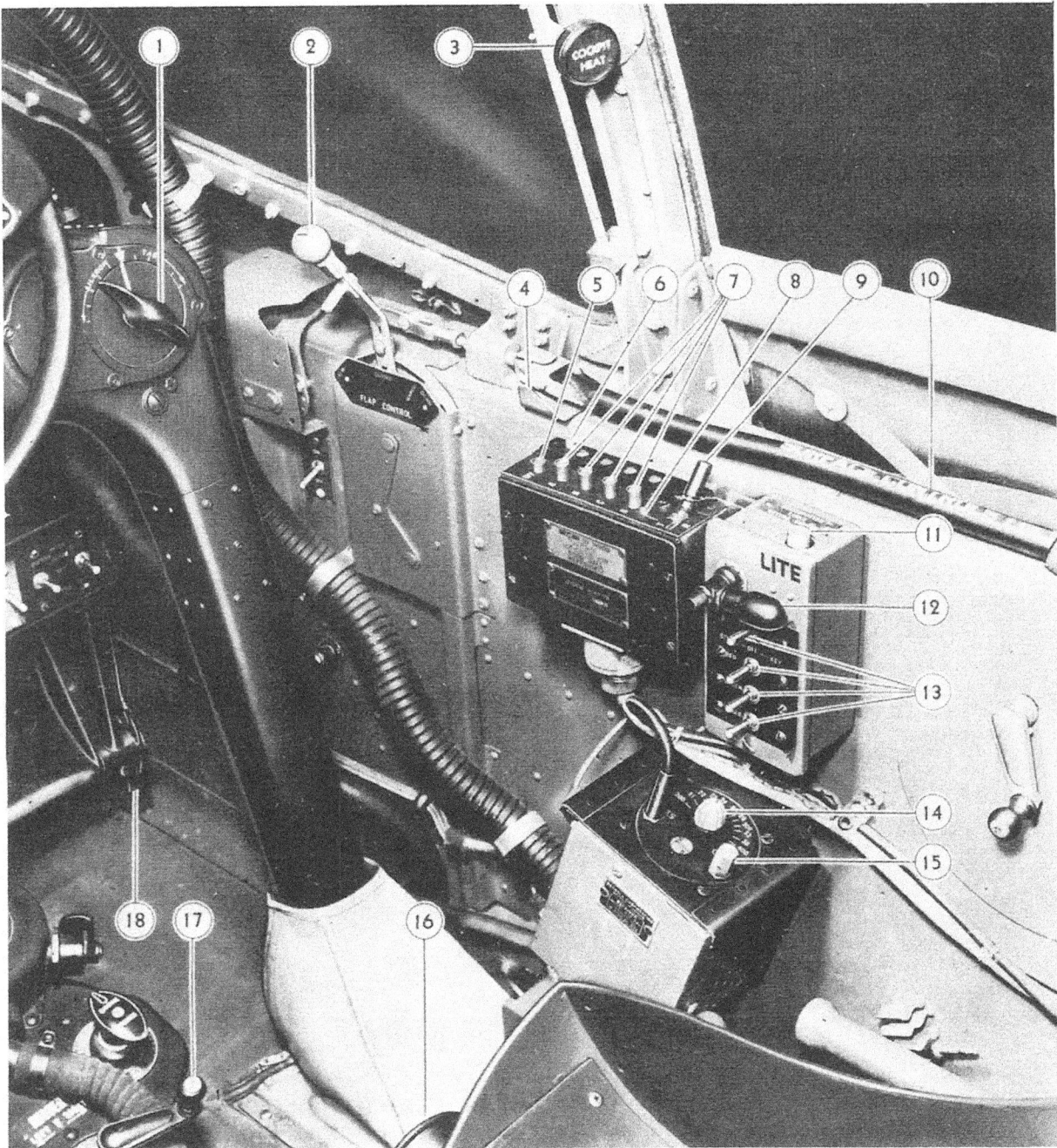

COCKPIT—RIGHT-HAND SIDE

1. Aileron tab control.
2. Flap control lever.
3. Cockpit heat control.
4. Surface controls lock guide angle.
5. Radio OFF push button.
6. Indicator light dimming lever.
7. Frequency selector push buttons.
8. Selector lock lever.
9. Selector switch.
10. Surface controls lock (stowed).
11. Recognition light keying switch.
12. Cockpit light.
13. Recognition light switches.
14. Detrola receiver tuning knob.
15. Detrola receiver volume control.
16. Pilot's relief tube.
17. Rudder trim tab control.
18. Rudder pedal adjustment lever.

MAIN SWITCH BOX

1. Ignition master switch.
2. Oil dilution switches.
3. Starter switch.
4. Engage switch.
5. Flourescent light switch.
6. Position light switches.
7. Landing light switches (left-hand only on P-38J, P-38L, and F-5B).
8. Voltmeter.
9. Inverter switch (P-38H).
10. Gunsight light rheostat (on control column of later airplanes).
11. Cockpit light rheostat.
12. Intercooler flap switches. (P-38J, P-38L, and F-5B. Circuit not in use on P-38H.)
13. Coolant flap override switches.
14. Pitot heat switch.
15. Battery switch.
16. Generator switch. (Two on instrument panel of later airplanes.)
17. Oil cooler flap switches.
18. Ignition switches.
19. Inverter warning light (P-38H).

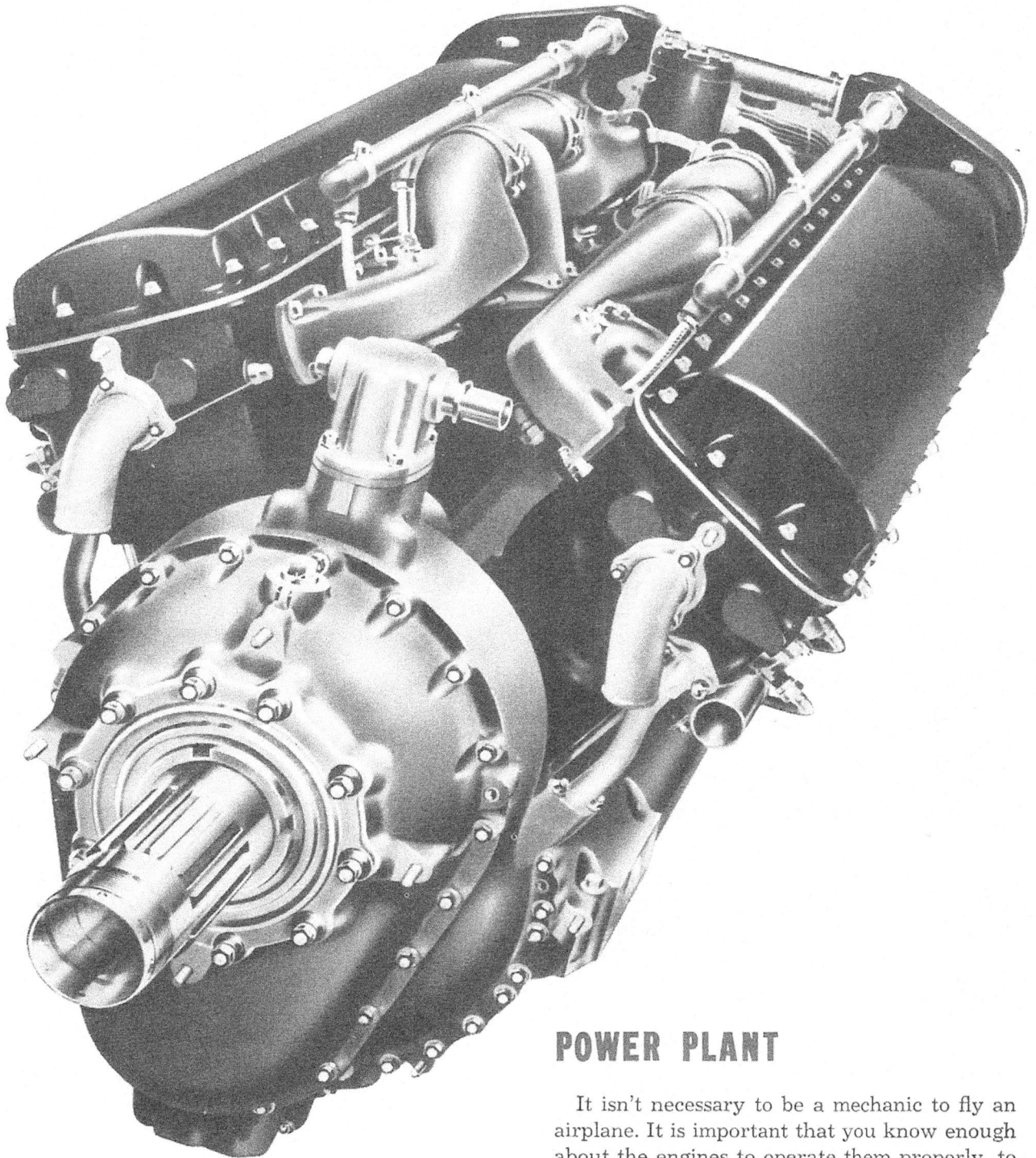

POWER PLANT

It isn't necessary to be a mechanic to fly an airplane. It is important that you know enough about the engines to operate them properly, to know their limitations, and to recognize trouble.

The P-38 has two 12-cylinder V-1710 liquid-cooled Allison engines. Know them, understand them, and treat them with respect. These engines are your life insurance.

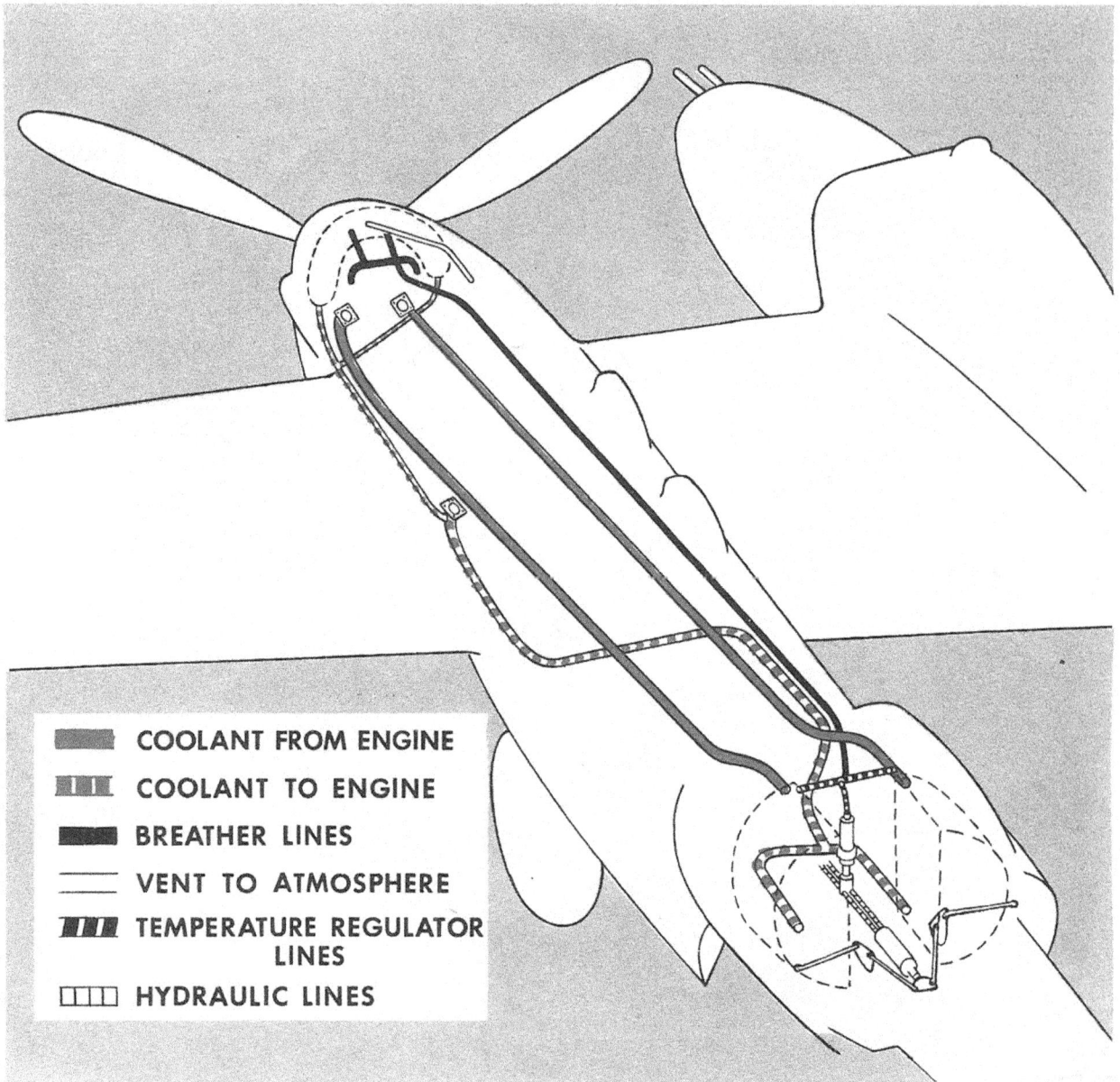

COOLANT FROM ENGINE

COOLANT TO ENGINE

BREATHER LINES

VENT TO ATMOSPHERE

TEMPERATURE REGULATOR LINES

HYDRAULIC LINES

COOLING SYSTEM

The engines are liquid cooled with a separate cooling system for each. The coolant is ethylene glycol. The ethylene glycol has the same function as water in the radiator of an automobile.

The coolant absorbs excess heat and dissipates it through radiators on the tail booms. The cooling radiators have hydraulically operated flaps. Changing the position of the coolant flaps varies the flow of air through the radiators. This regulates the coolant temperature.

Coolant Temperature

MINIMUM COOLANT TEMPERATURE IS 85°C;

DESIRED 105°C TO 115°C;

MAXIMUM 125°C.

P-38 Series Through P-38G-10

Operate the coolant flaps by levers located on the engine control stand at the base of the left window.

The coolant flap control levers have 3 positions: Push them forward to open the flaps, and rearward to close them. The center position is neutral. You can stop the flaps in any desired position by returning the levers to neutral.

Look over your shoulder to check the position of the flaps.

If the hydraulic system fails, you can operate the coolant flaps by the auxiliary hand pump, **but not by the emergency extension system.**

P-38G-15 Through P-38-L

Two coolant override switches on the main switch box replace the coolant flap control levers.

The switches have 3 positions: OFF, FULL OPEN, and FULL CLOSED.

Place the switches in the OFF position and the coolant flaps operate automatically, maintaining the coolant temperature between 100°C and 120°C.

Operate the coolant flaps manually in the FULL OPEN or FULL CLOSED position. Use these positions if the automatic OFF position fails to maintain the desired temperature. You cannot set the coolant flaps to any position other than full open or full closed when using the coolant override switches.

TO OPEN THE COOLANT FLAPS:

Place the override switches in **FULL OPEN.**

TO CLOSE THE COOLANT FLAPS:

Place the override switches in **FULL CLOSE.**
If the hydraulic system fails completely, the coolant flaps assume a streamlined position.

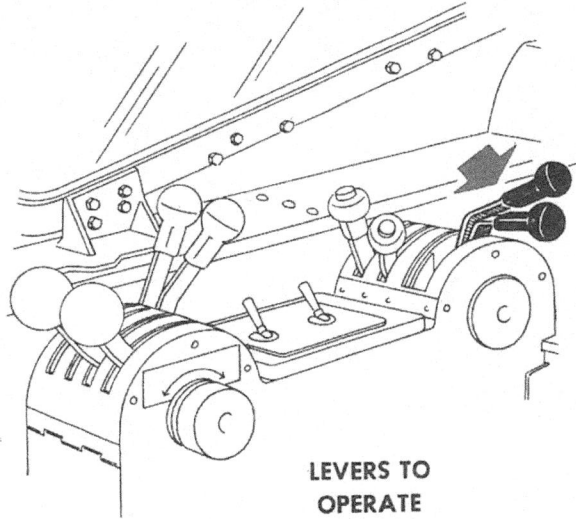

LEVERS TO OPERATE COOLANT FLAPS

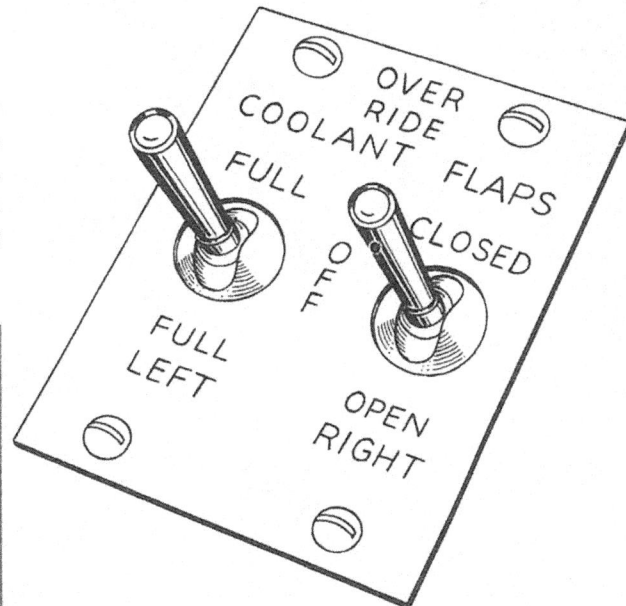

COOLANT OVERRIDE SWITCHES

OIL SYSTEM

Legend:

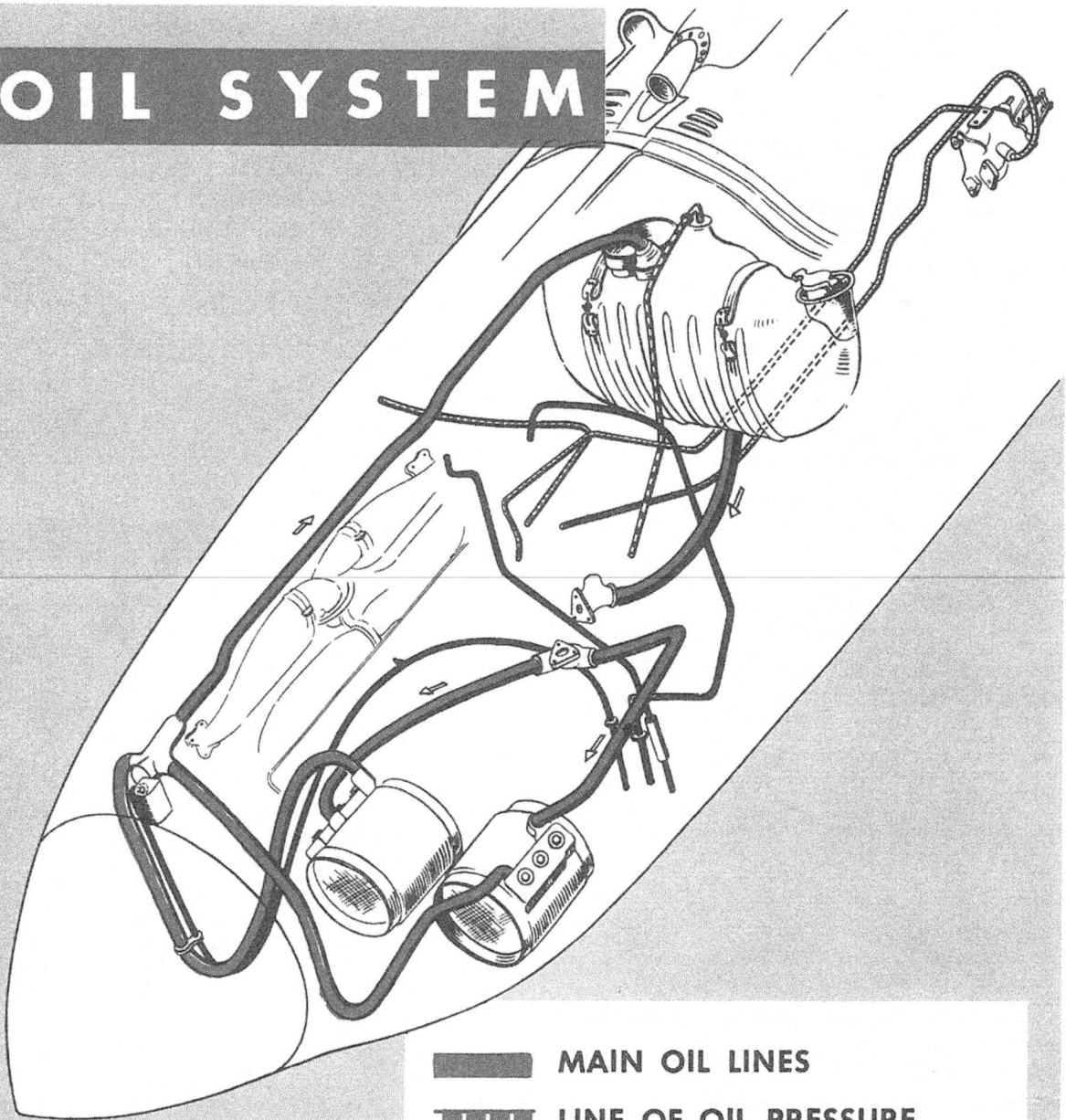

- ▬▬▬ MAIN OIL LINES
- ▥▥▥ LINE OF OIL PRESSURE GAGE
- ▬▬▬ BREATHER LINES
- ▦▦▦ VENT LINES
- ▫▫▫ SUPERCHARGER REGULATOR OIL LINE (Early airplanes only)

RESTRICTED

Oil Temperature

Oil is cooled by air passing through oil radiators in front of the nacelles. Oil cooler shutters on the bottom of the nacelles vary the flow of air through the radiators.

You can see the oil shutters by leaning forward in the cockpit and looking at the bottom of the engine cowl.

Minimum oil temperature is 40°C; **desired,** 70°C to 80°C; and **maximum, 95°C.**

P-38 Series Through G-15

Operate the oil cooler shutters by two spring-loaded toggle switches located on the front face of the main switch box. The switches have 3 positions: OFF, OPEN, and CLOSE. Place the switches in the OPEN or CLOSE position, and when the shutters have reached the desired position, return the switches to OFF.

An oil shutter position indicator is on the instrument panel.

P-38H Through P-38L

The oil shutter switches have 4 positions: AUTOMATIC, OFF, OPEN, and CLOSE. Place the switches in the AUTOMATIC position, and the oil temperature is automatically regulated between 75°C and 95°C. Manual operation is the same as outlined for the oil cooler flap switches not equipped with the AUTOMATIC position.

The oil shutters are on the sides of the nacelles instead of the bottom. You can see them from the cockpit. For that reason this series does not have oil shutter position indicators.

Oil Pressure

You must maintain proper oil pressure to operate the engines efficiently. Here are a few general rules that will help you:

Always check the pressure and temperature relationship.

With low pressure and high temperature—open the oil shutters; the temperature will go down and the pressure up.

With high pressure and low temperature—close the oil shutters; the temperature will go up and the pressure down.

If the pressure is either high or low and the oil temperature is normal, reduce power and land.

You can bring the plane home under reduced power if the oil pressure does not go below 40 psi.

If the oil pressure is below 40 psi and the temperature is above the red line, cut the mixture control and feather the propeller of the engine. Single engine flight is no problem, whereas if you continue to use the bad engine it can develop into a serious fire hazard.

Oil Dilution

The oil dilution system allows gasoline to flow into the oil system. Diluting the oil in cold weather makes it easier to start the engines.

Important: Oil dilution is not effective if the oil temperature is above 50°C and coolant temperature above 70°C. Stop the engines and allow them to cool before proceeding.

To dilute the oil:

1. Run engines at 1000 rpm.

2. Move oil dilution switches to ON position and hold for required time. The oil pressure will drop.

Oil Dilution in Minutes	
Anticipated Outside Air Temperature	Dilution Time
4°C to —12°C.................3 min.	
—12°C to —29°C.................5 min.	
—29°C to —46°C.................8 min.	

3. Move mixture control to IDLE CUT-OFF.

4. When engines stop, release oil dilution switches.

Note: If oil has been diluted the night before, check to see that oil pressure is up and constant before takeoff.

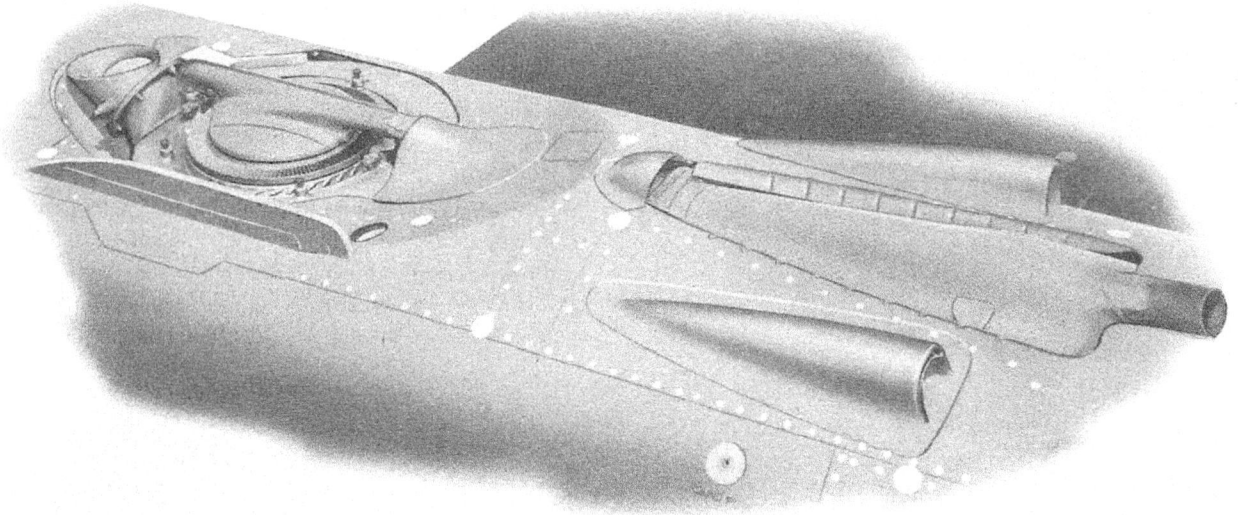

SUPERCHARGERS AND THROTTLE

The P-38 is equipped with two exhaust-driven turbo-superchargers. They are on the top surfaces of the tail booms aft of the engine nacelles. A supercharger is to an engine as an oxygen mask is to you at high altitudes. Superchargers increase the density of air in the cylinders to provide maximum performance of the engines at high altitudes.

There are no additional controls to operate the superchargers. They are mechanically connected to the throttles and operate automatically when you advance the throttles.

In the two-thirds to wide open range of the throttles, engine response is sluggish. This lag is the time required for the superchargers to reach their new speed.

Note: Operate the throttles the same way you operate conventional throttles.

As you advance the throttles beyond two-thirds of the quadrant, a valve on the exhaust is gradually closed. This valve is similar in operation to the butterfly valve on the carburetor. It is called the waste gate. The more the waste gate closes, the faster the turbo wheel spins; the faster the turbo wheel spins, the greater the compression of air to the cylinders. The turbo speed increases with an increase of altitude and throttle. The critical altitude at which the superchargers will maintain sea level ratings for the engines is determined by the rpm limitation of the turbo. If you exceed this rpm limitation by using more than the prescribed manifold pressure, the turbo overspeeds and serious material damage can result.

Decrease the allowable manifold pressure one inch per thousand feet above 25,000 feet on P-38F and P-38G series. Start to decrease manifold pressure above 30,000 feet on P-38H and P-38J series. This keeps the turbos within their rpm limitations.

Turbo Overspeed Warning Lights

Turbo overspeed warning lights are installed on the instrument panel of the P-38H and P-38J.

The warning lights flicker when the turbos are reaching their rpm limitation. They burn steadily when the rpm limitation is reached. Their intensity increases as this limitation is exceeded.

While the lights flicker you have a safety margin and can reduce the turbo speed before serious damage results. Reduce the engine power before the lights burn steadily.

Manifold Pressure Regulator

P-38L's and later series of the P-38J have a manifold pressure regulator which automatically controls the carburetor butterfly valve. It provides a constant manifold pressure for any given throttle setting during climb, descent and maneuvers. It also prevents the manifold pressure from exceeding its limits in a dive.

Turbo Supercharger Regulator

P-38L's and later P-38J's have a turbo regulator incorporating an overspeed governor that prevents the turbo wheel from running at speeds beyond the safety limit. These models do not have turbo overspeed warning lights. The regulator is automatic. You don't have any control over its operation.

Intercoolers

The temperature of air passing through the turbo-superchargers increases because of compression.

The intercoolers cool the hot air from the supercharger before it enters the carburetors. Previous to the P-38J, the intercoolers were in the leading edge of the wing and the pilot did not control them.

The intercoolers on later airplanes are in the nacelles. The space inside the leading edge of the wing, outboard of the nacelles, is used for outer wing fuel tanks and a left leading edge landing light. In the nacelles, the intercoolers have greater protection from enemy gunfire, are accessible to mechanics for maintenance, and you control their operation.

The P-38J and P-38L series are provided with intercooler shutters on the bottom of the engine nacelles. By opening or closing the shutters, you can control the carburetor air temperature.

Operate the intercooler shutters by two toggle switches on the main switch box. The switches have 3 positions: OPEN, OFF, and CLOSE. You can stop the shutters in any desired intermediate position by returning the switches to OFF. They operate in the same manner as the oil shutters on all P-38 series previous to the J.

Carburetor Heat

The turbo-superchargers automatically provide carburetor heat. It is possible, however, to encounter carburetor icing during icing conditions and extreme cold when operating at low power.

If carburetor icing occurs, increase power to at least 30″ manifold pressure. This increases the temperature of the carburetor air and clears away the ice.

Keep the carburetor air temperature between 20°C and 35°C.

Maximum carburetor air temperature is 45°C.

Note: With extremely high outside air temperature, carburetor air temperature exceeds 45°C during ground operation.

Carburetor temperature on P-38J and P-38L is controlled by adjustment of the intercooler shutters.

Carburetor Air Filters

Use carburetor air filters during dusty ground operation. On earlier P-38 series the air filters operate automatically. They remain open on the ground and close when the wheels are retracted.

When operated manually, do not use them once you are off the ground and in clear air. The use of carburetor air filters **reduces the critical altitude and range of the airplane.**

The carburetor air filter manual control is to the left, behind the pilot's seat. On P-38J's and P-38L's the control is on the engine control stand in place of the coolant shutter controls.

MIXTURE CONTROLS

The engines have pressure type carburetors that maintain an automatic fuel mixture at any altitude. The mixture controls have 4 main settings: EMERGENCY RICH, AUTO RICH, AUTO LEAN, and IDLE CUT-OFF.

Use these positions as follows:

Idle Cut-off

For starting and stopping the engines. The controls are left in this position when the engines are not running.

Auto Lean

For economical cruising at any altitude.

Auto Rich

For takeoff, climbing, cruising at any altitude, and landing.

Emergency Rich

For emergency use, when the automatic feature of the carburetor fails.

CLOVER LEAF VALVE SETTING OF NOTCHES BETWEEN IDLE CUT-OFF AND EMERGENCY RICH

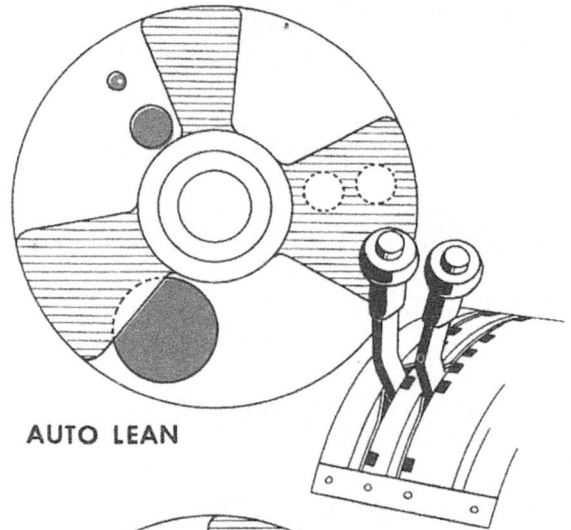

AUTO LEAN

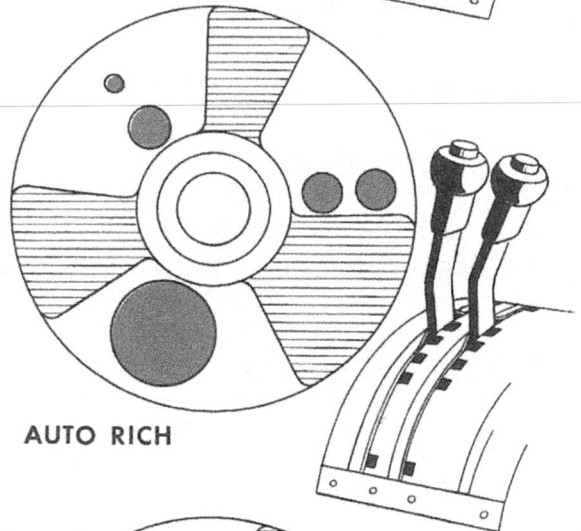

AUTO RICH

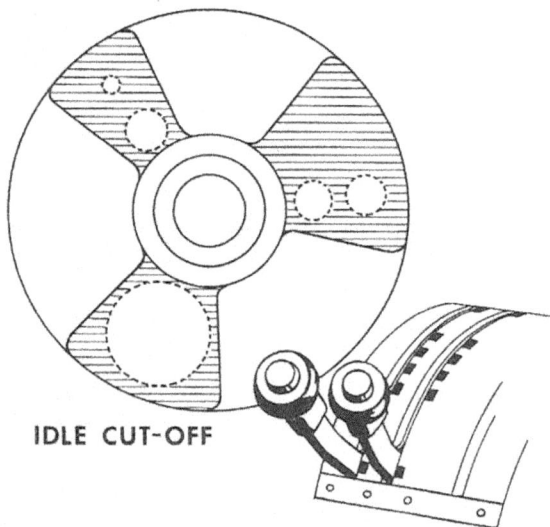

IDLE CUT-OFF

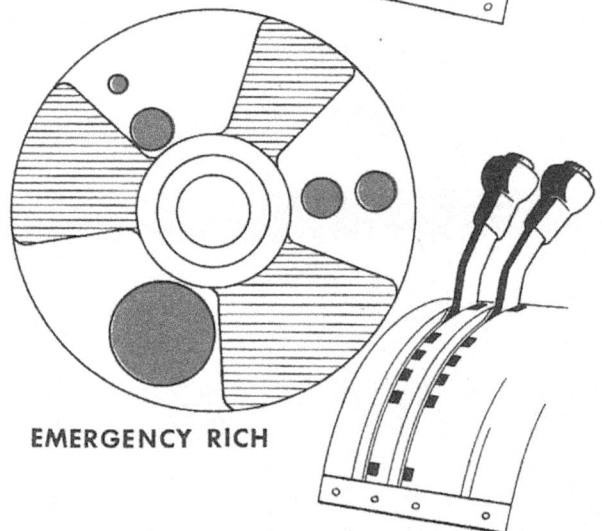

EMERGENCY RICH

CURTISS ELECTRIC PROPELLER

You have been using the hydromatic constant speed propeller; now you have two Curtiss electric propellers. You know the principle of operation. The angle of the blades is controlled while in flight to provide maximum efficiency and maintain constant engine speed under varying operating conditions.

The propellers are counter-rotating. The propeller on the right engine rotates clockwise while the one on the left rotates counter-clockwise. This eliminates torque and provides the airplane with excellent climbing and diving characteristics. That means less work for you.

There is a control which gives you either automatic constant speed or manual fixed pitch. There is also an emergency control enabling you to feather either propeller in case of engine failure.

Remember

Increase rpm first, then manifold pressure.
Decrease manifold pressure first, then rpm.

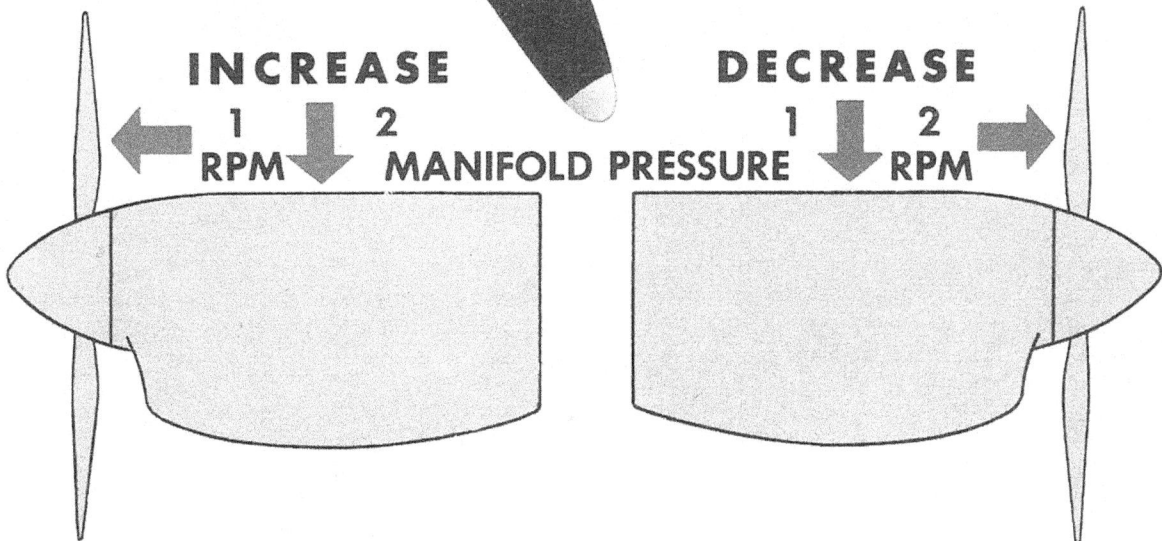

INCREASE
1 RPM 2 MANIFOLD PRESSURE

DECREASE
1 MANIFOLD PRESSURE 2 RPM

Propeller Circuit Breaker

Curtiss electric propellers have circuit breakers which protect them against electrical overloads. Keep circuit breakers ON at all times.

The P-38 has push button type circuit breakers forward of the engine control stand. They operate like a pop-out cigarette lighter in an automobile. When an overload occurs in the electrical system, these buttons become hot and pop out, disclosing a red and white band. To reset the circuit breakers, let them cool for 10 or 15 seconds; then push the buttons in and hold them down for about 15 seconds.

If a continuous overload occurs, repeatedly throwing the circuit breakers into the OFF position, allow sufficient time for the circuit to cool; then hold the switches in the ON position. The circuit breakers will carry extremely high loads.

Warning!

Keep the circuit breakers ON at all times. Check to be sure they are ON before take-off.

TO RESET CIRCUIT BREAKERS, PUSH BUTTONS IN AFTER 10 OR 15 SECONDS COOLING PERIOD

Automatic Constant Speed

In AUTOMATIC, a governor and a relay maintain a constant engine speed within the limits of the control lever operation. The control levers are on the engine control stand. They operate the propellers in the same way they operate the propellers on the AT-6 and AT-9. Pull them back and you decrease the rpm. Push them forward and you increase the rpm. For takeoff **the control levers are full forward.** Change them to provide the correct rpm for climb, cruise, and other maneuvers.

A vernier knob is on the side of the engine control stand. You can obtain fine adjustment of the right hand propeller governor with the vernier.

Synchronize propellers by ear, using the tachometers, and the vernier. Use the friction control to prevent the throttles and propeller

governors from vibrating out of position. Remember the rule:

"Increase rpm before increasing manifold pressure. Decrease manifold pressure before decreasing rpm."

Manual Fixed Pitch

In manual FIXED PITCH the propellers operate as fixed pitch propellers. This position is used to conserve the battery or if the automatic constant speed control fails to operate.

Use the manual FIXED PITCH position to conserve the battery on extended flights when altitude, airspeed, and power remain constant for a long period of time.

Manual Operation

1. Move selector switch to FIXED PITCH.
2. Hold selector switch momentarily to INCREASE RPM or DECREASE RPM (as required).
3. When you obtain desired rpm setting, return selector switch to FIXED PITCH.

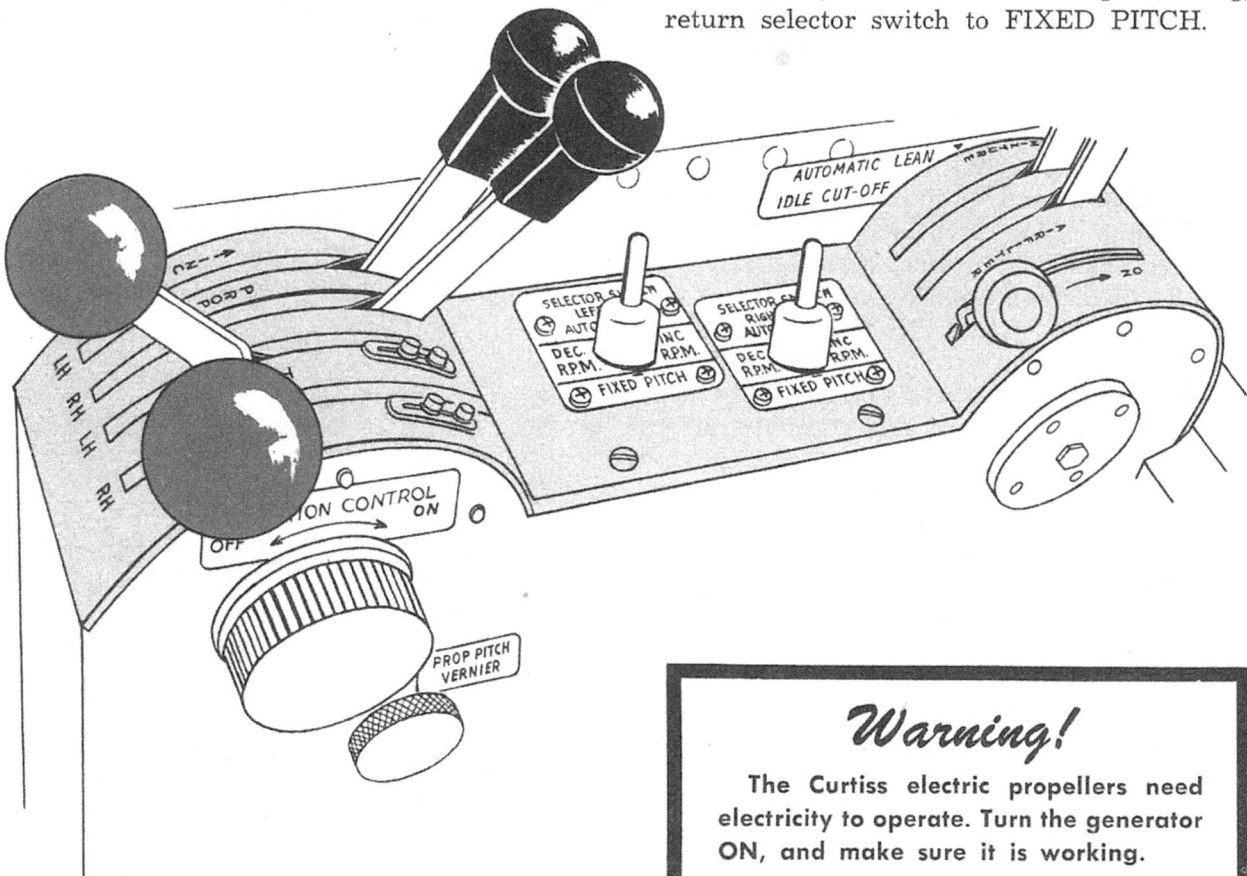

Warning!

The Curtiss electric propellers need electricity to operate. Turn the generator ON, and make sure it is working.

FEATHERING

Feathering a propeller permits the stopping of a disabled and vibrating engine. It decreases the drag of the propeller and increases the single engine performance of the airplane.

The feathering control switches have 2 positions: NORMAL and FEATHER. To feather a propeller, **all you have to do** is place the feathering control switch at FEATHER. The feathering switch by-passes the AUTOMATIC and manual FIXED PITCH switches. Regardless of the position of the selector switches, the propeller blades turn to the feather angle and stop when the feathering switch is placed to FEATHER.

Featheritis

If you develop engine trouble in flight, don't jump for the feathering switch.

1. Don't get in a hurry to land.

2. You have a good single engine airplane under you.

3. Go over your checklist. Feathering may not be necessary.

4. Definitely determine which engine is bad. Wrong engines have been feathered.

5. Check the airplane thoroughly. Try to determine the cause.

Note: You may be out of gas. Switch to fullest tank. Remember, don't be in a hurry, don't get excited. You're not going to fall out of the sky.

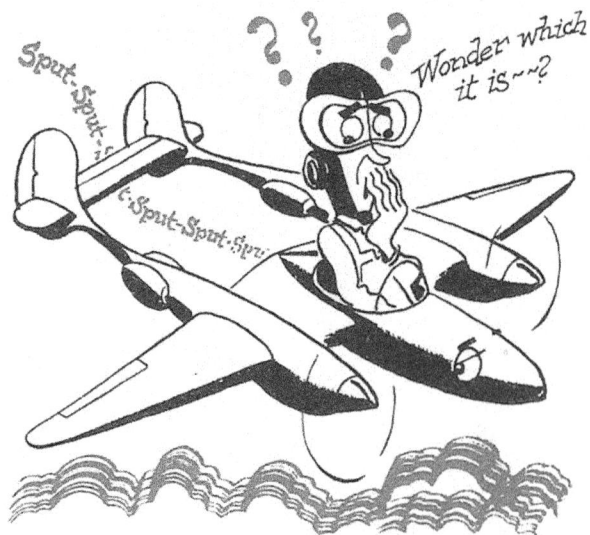

Feathering Indicator Lights

On later P-38's, feathering indicator lights located above the feathering switches help you feather the propeller of a bad engine. If your right engine fails, you push hard left rudder to correct yaw. The right feathering light then glows, indicating that the right propeller is the one to be feathered. The reverse is true if the left engine fails.

Unfeathering

1. Return feather switch to NORMAL.
2. Hold propeller selector switch to IN-CREASE RPM until tachometer reading is 1000 rpm.
3. Move propeller selector switch to AUTO-MATIC. This brings the rpm up to the setting of the propeller governor lever.

Overspeeding Propeller

An overspeeding propeller is one which allows the engine to overspeed. If you have an overspeeding prop, immediately retard the throttle to 3000 rpm. Then do the following:

1. Check to be sure propeller selector switches are in AUTOMATIC.
2. Make certain circuit breakers are ON.
3. Try to reduce rpm by propeller governor.
4. Hold selector switch in DECREASE RPM position.

If this fails to reduce the rpm, place feather switch to FEATHER and return it to NORMAL when desired rpm is reached. Be careful not to reduce the rpm too much when using this method.

Warning Lights

Propeller warning lights are installed on the P-38H only. They indicate when the propeller circuits are not properly set for takeoff and landing. They blink on and off when the circuit breakers are open, or when the propeller selector switches are not set in AUTOMATIC. However, these lights do not warn of an improperly set propeller pitch control.

PROPELLER PREFLIGHT CHECK

Check to see that propeller circuit breaker switches are ON.

Manual Operation Check

1. Propeller selector switch to manual FIXED PITCH.

2. With the engine running at approximately 2300 rpm, put the selector switch in DE-CREASE RPM until you have a drop of 200 rpm.

3. Move selector switch to INCREASE RPM until tachometer reading returns to 2300 rpm.

Automatic Operation Check

1. Propeller selector switches in AUTO-MATIC.

2. Propeller governors in the full forward takeoff position.

3. Open throttles to obtain 2300 rpm.

4. Pull the propeller governors back until you get a reduction of 200 rpm.

5. Return the propeller governors to the full forward takeoff position, noting that they return to 2300 rpm. If they do, the propellers are operating normally and are ready for flight.

DON'T USE AILERON AGAINST THE TURN.
THIS HAS A BLANKETING ACTION ON
THE RUDDERS.

PROPELLER CHECKLIST

Generator Switch

Be sure it is ON and working properly. The Curtiss electric propeller needs electricity to operate.

Circuit Breakers

On at all times.

Feather Switch

In NORMAL position.

Takeoff

Propeller selector switches in AUTOMATIC. Propeller control governors full forward in takeoff position.

Cruising

Selector switches in AUTOMATIC. Obtain desired rpm with propeller governors.

Landing

Selector switches in AUTOMATIC. Set to 2600 rpm with governors.

After Landing

Before stopping the engines, move the governors full forward to takeoff position.

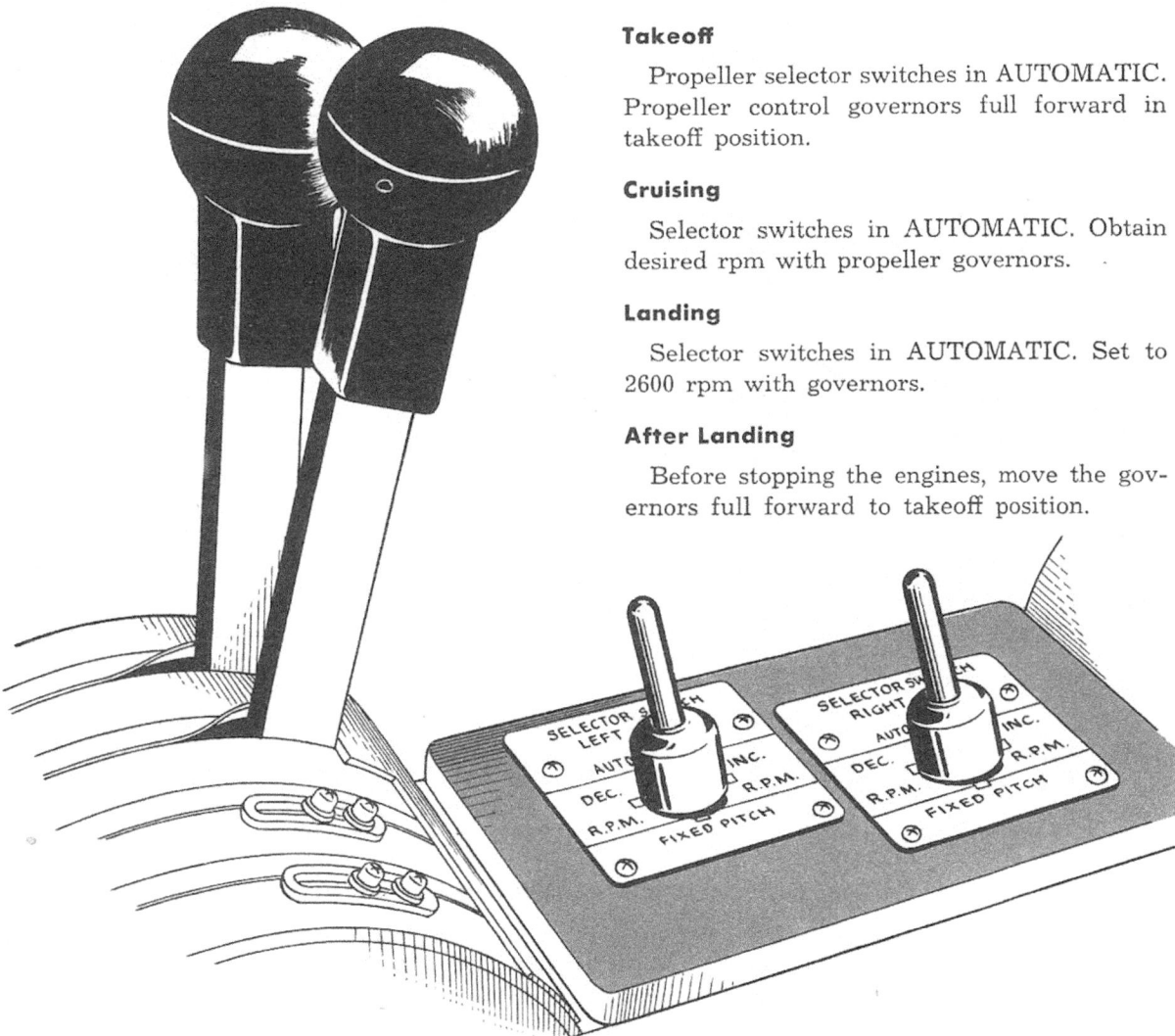

FUEL SYSTEM

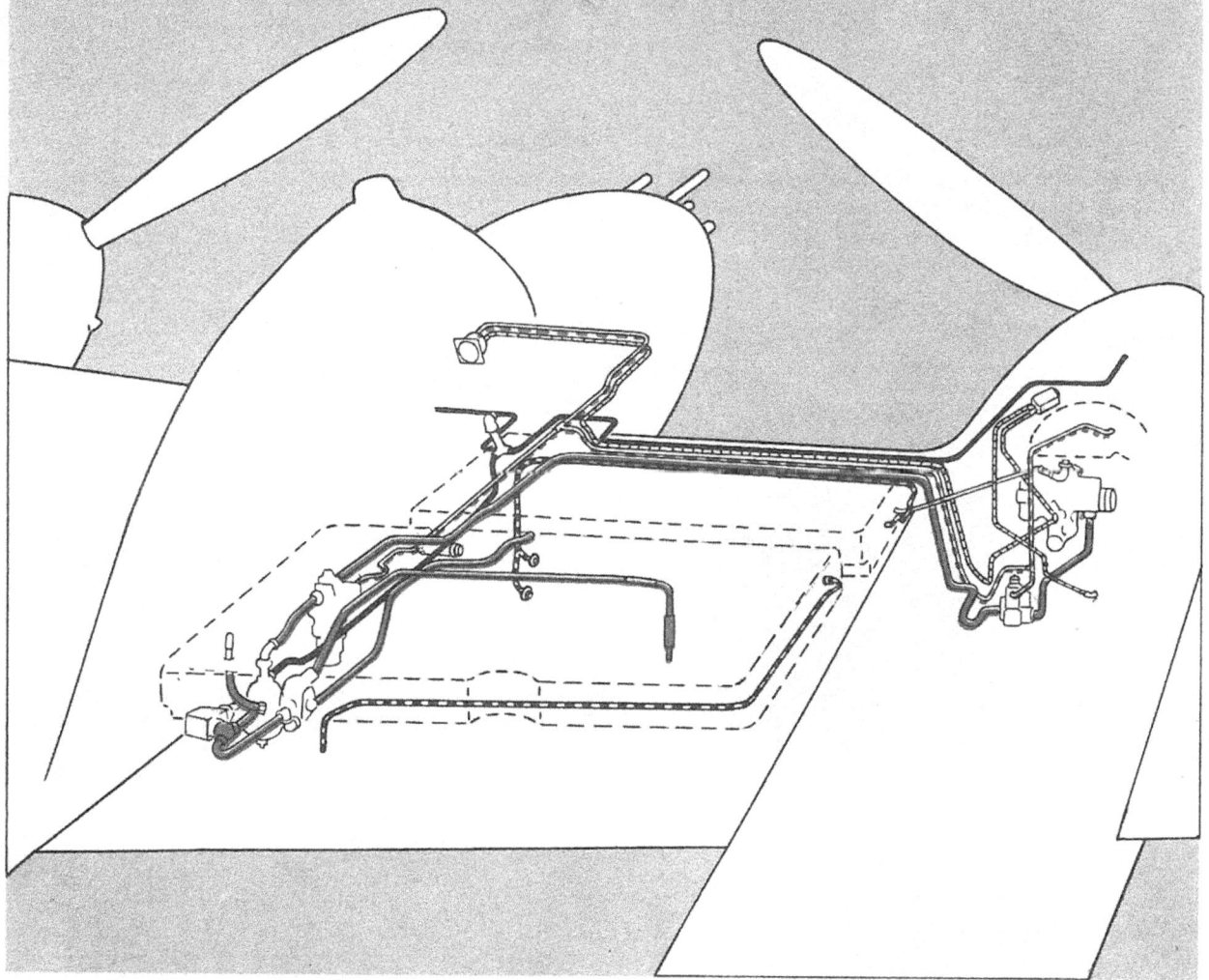

- ▬▬▬ MAIN FUEL LINES
- ▬❚❚❚▬ FUEL PRESSURE BALANCE LINES
- ▬▬▬ ENGINE PRIMER LINES
- ❚❚❚❚❚ FUEL PRESSURE LINES
- ═══ VAPOR RETURN LINES
- ❚❚❚❚❚ FUEL TANK VENT LINES

Fuel Pressure

Fuel is supplied to each engine by one engine driven pump and one electric booster pump. The engine pumps maintain a normal fuel pressure of 16 psi to 18 psi up to 12,000 feet. Above 12,000 feet, normal fuel pressure is maintained by the booster pumps.

Electric Fuel Booster Pumps

The electric booster pumps serve for starting the engines, takeoff and landing, flying above 12,000 feet, or in case the engine driven pumps fail.

The electric booster pumps are controlled by 2 switches on the left side of the cockpit floor.

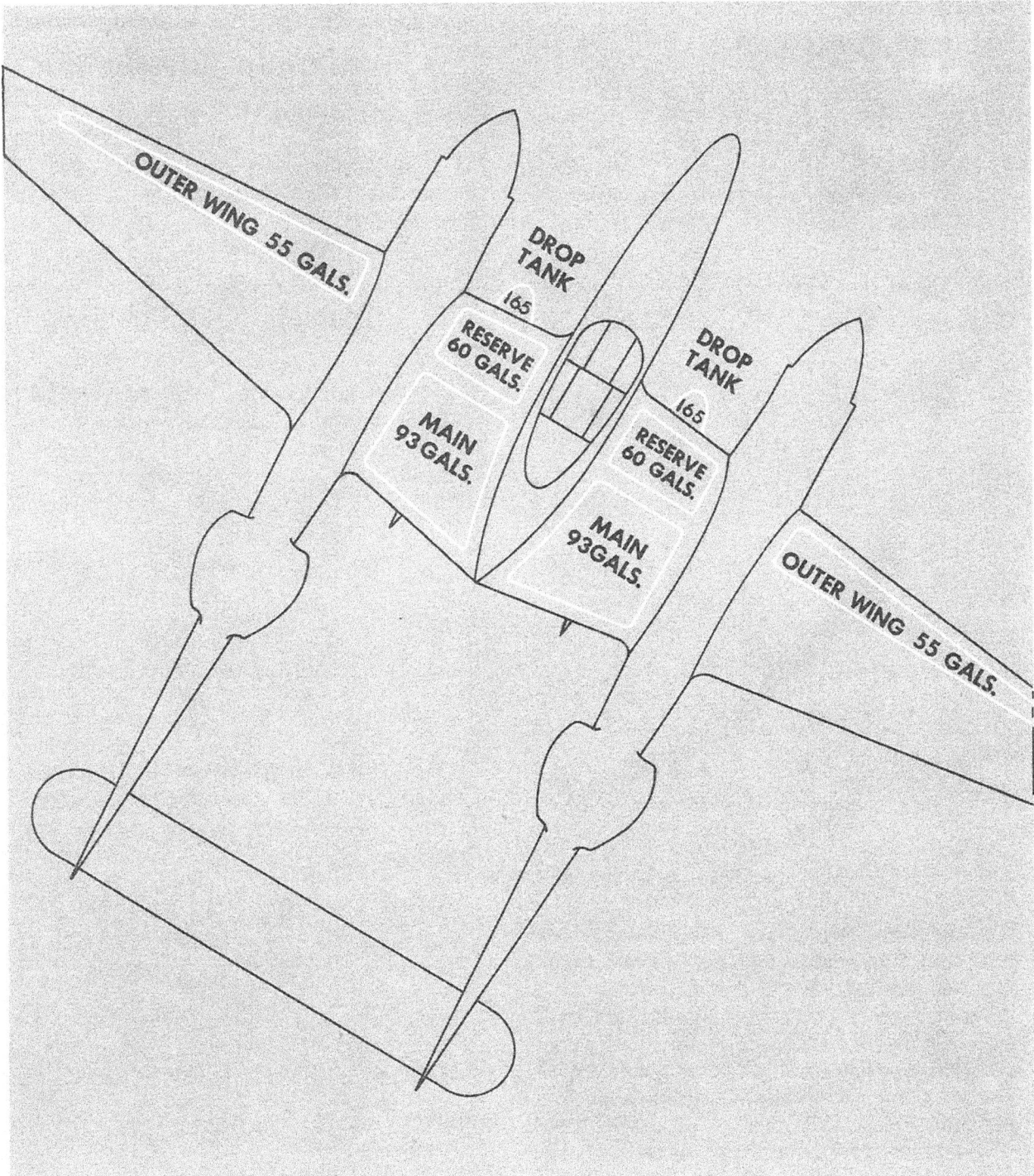

OUTER WING 55 GALS.

DROP
TANK

165

RESERVE
60 GALS.

DROP
TANK

165

MAIN
93 GALS.

RESERVE
60 GALS.

MAIN
93 GALS.

OUTER WING 55 GALS.

FUEL TANKS

P-38 Series Through P-38J-10

There are 4 self-sealing wing fuel tanks. The
2 front reserve tanks hold 60 gallons each. The
2 rear main tanks hold 93 gallons each.

P-38J-15 Through P-38L

These series have in addition to the 4 standard fuel tanks, 2 outer wing tanks with a
capacity of 55 gallons each.

DROP TANKS

To operate drop tank (or bomb) release

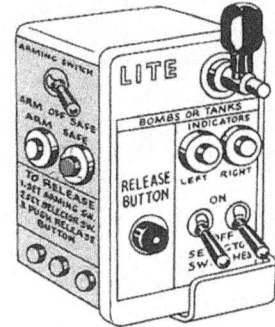

Place arming switch to ARM or SAFE. Indicator lights show the position of the arming switch.

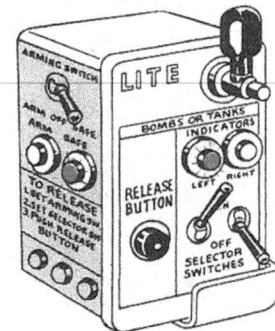

Place selector switch ON for tank (or bomb) to be dropped. Indicator lights show which selector switch is in the ON position.

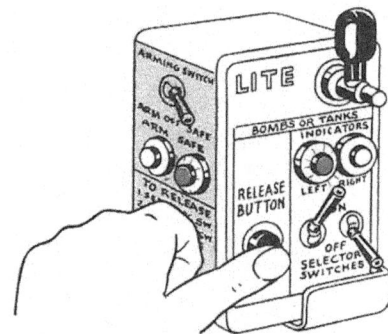

Press the release button.

Manual releases are provided as a substitute for the electrical release. Check your airplane for their location and operation.

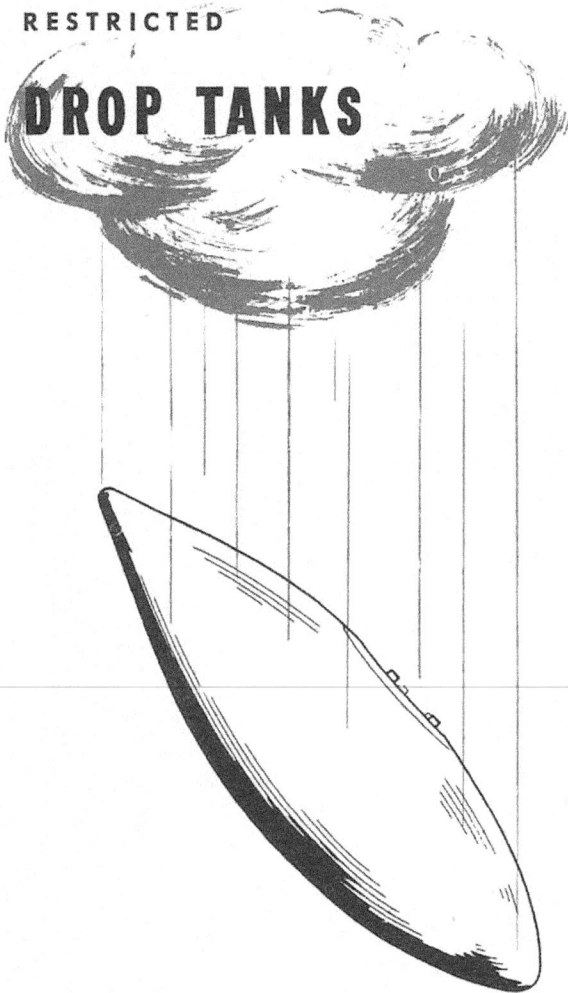

Beneath each wing is a shackle for carrying an external drop tank (or bomb). Sway braces are added for carrying 330-gallon drop tanks.

You may have to drop the external tanks to lighten your load if an engine fails, or to give you greater maneuverability in combat. Before you drop them, turn the fuel selector valves to the wing tanks.

If you release empty drop tanks at high speeds, they will damage the flaps. Some P-38's have a special brace to prevent this and you can drop the tanks, empty or full, at any speed.

You can drop the tanks (or bombs) individually or both at the same time. The release box is on the left side of the cockpit just below the window.

4-WAY FUEL SELECTORS ▶

L.H. TANK SELECTOR

R.H. TANK SELECTOR

L.H. TANK SELECTOR

R.H. TANK SELECTOR

◀ **5-WAY FUEL SELECTORS**

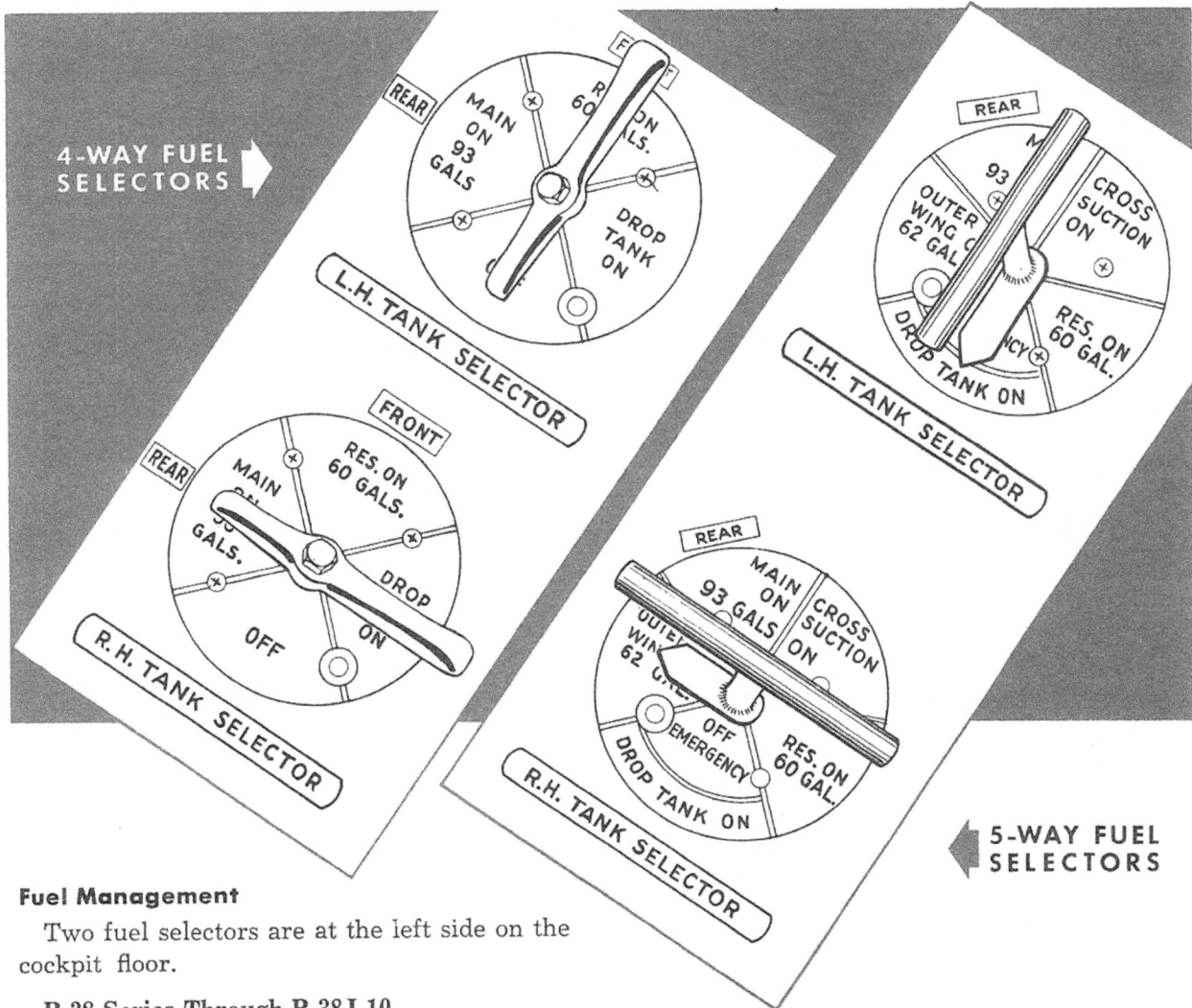

Fuel Management

Two fuel selectors are at the left side on the cockpit floor.

P-38 Series Through P-38J-10
1. RES (reserve)
2. DROP TANK
3. OFF
4. MAIN

P-38J-20 Through P-38L
1. MAIN
2. CROSS SUCTION
3. RES (reserve)
4. OFF–DROP TANK
5. OUTER WING

The P-38J-15 also has a 5-position selector. However the outer wing tanks have separate selectors. (There are two toggle switches in back of the electric booster pump control box.) OFF and DROP TANK occupy separate positions on the fuel selector face.

Take-off and fly on the reserve tanks for the first 15 minutes. This is necessary because of a bleed-back of unmetered fuel from the carburetor to the reserve tanks. If you use other tanks first, the unmetered fuel goes back to the full reserve tanks. This causes the fuel to siphon out of the reserve tanks. Stop the siphoning by switching to RES (reserve).

Use fuel in the following sequence:
1. Reserve for the first 15 minutes.
2. External drop tanks (if carried).
3. Outer wing tanks (if installed).
4. Main.
5. Reserve.

Outer Wing Tanks

The outer wing tanks have their own booster pumps. When you are using fuel from these tanks turn the regular booster pumps to OFF.

To Operate Outer Wing Tanks,
P-38J-15

Turn the outer wing tank selectors to ON, and turn the regular fuel selectors to OFF.

P-38J-20 Through P-38L

Turn the fuel selectors to OUTER WING (outer wing tanks) and turn the booster pumps to OFF.

Fuel Quantity Gages

Two fuel quantity gages on the instrument panel indicate only for the reserve and main tanks. The fuel quantity in the drop tanks and outer wing tanks must be estimated by hourly fuel consumption.

Fuel test lights for the outer wing tanks are located forward of the engine control stand. If you are using the outer wing tanks, the warning lights glow when there are approximately 10 to 15 gallons left. Later airplanes have a low level test button to check fuel level in the outer wing tanks before you turn the tanks on.

Crossfeed System

An electrical crossfeed system makes it possible to feed fuel to either engine from any tank except outer wing tanks. Use the crossfeed system when prolonged single engine flight makes it necessary to draw fuel from the dead engine side, or when you want to operate both engines from the fuel in one drop tank.

Crossfeed Operation,
P-38 Series Through P-38J-10

1. Turn the fuel selector to the tank you want to draw fuel from.
2. Turn crossfeed switch to CROSSFEED.
3. Turn the other fuel selector to OFF.

Note: Keep your hand on the fuel selector until you are sure both engines are drawing fuel from the desired tank.

P-38J-15 Through P-38L

1. Turn fuel selector to tank you want to draw fuel from.
2. Turn the other selector to CROSS SUCTION.

CROSS SUCTION or CROSSFEED does not operate for the outer wing tanks.

FUEL CAPACITY

	4 WING TANKS	6 WING TANKS
NO DROP TANKS	306 GALS.	416 GALS.
TWO 165-GAL. TANKS	636 GALS.	746 GALS.
TWO 330-GAL. TANKS	966 GALS.	1076 GALS.

FUEL CONSUMPTION

The following figures vary according to the load, trim, and condition of the airplane you are flying. Learn to time the fuel consumption of each tank. Under normal operating conditions, you use approximately 1 gallon a minute per engine. Never run a tank dry.

Fuel Consumption P-38H, P-38J, and P-38L
GRADE 100

POWER SETTINGS	RPM	HG.	MIXTURE	CONSUMPTION/HR./ENGINE
TAKEOFF AND MILITARY	3000	54"	AUTO-RICH	162 GALS.
WAR EMERGENCY	3000	60"	AUTO-RICH	180 GALS.
NORMAL RATED	2600	44"	AUTO-RICH	115 GALS.
MAXIMUM CRUISE	2300	35"	AUTO-LEAN	60 GALS.

Fuel Consumption P-38F and P-38G
GRADE 100

POWER SETTINGS	RPM	HG.	MIXTURE	CONSUMPTION/HR./ENGINE
TAKEOFF AND MILITARY	3000	47"	AUTO-RICH	148 GALS.
WAR EMERGENCY	3000	47"	AUTO-RICH	148 GALS.
NORMAL RATED	2600	41"	AUTO-RICH	110 GALS.
MAXIMUM CRUISE	2300	30"	AUTO-LEAN	53 GALS.

If you accidentally run a tank dry and the engine stops, do the following:
1. Pull back the throttle.
2. Turn selector valve to tank with fuel.
3. Turn fuel booster pump ON.
4. Slowly ease throttle forward. This prevents backfiring and an overspeeding propeller.

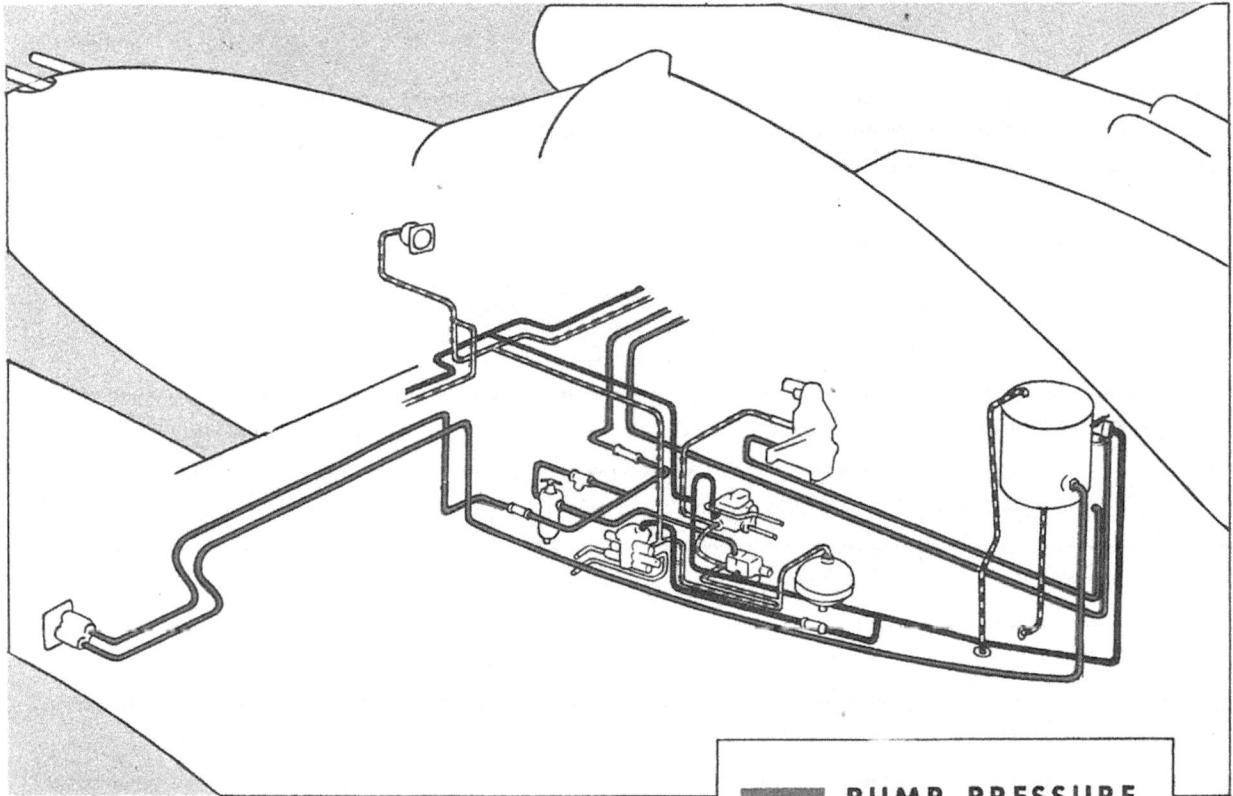

THE HYDRAULIC SYSTEM

The hydraulic system operates the landing gear, wheel well doors, wing flaps, and coolant shutters. The brakes are operated by a separate hydraulic system.

Hydraulic pressure is maintained by engine-driven pumps mounted one on each engine. Normal hydraulic pressure is between 1100 psi and 1400 psi. In later series a surge up to 1600 psi is permissible if it drops back to 1500 psi or less.

The system operates all the hydraulic equipment (except the brakes) using power from the engine-driven pumps and fluid from the **top half of the main hydraulic reservoir.**

Auxiliary System

The auxiliary system operates the same equipment and uses the same lines as the normal system. The difference is that the hand hydraulic pump furnishes the power, and the fluid comes from the **bottom of the main hydraulic reservoir.**

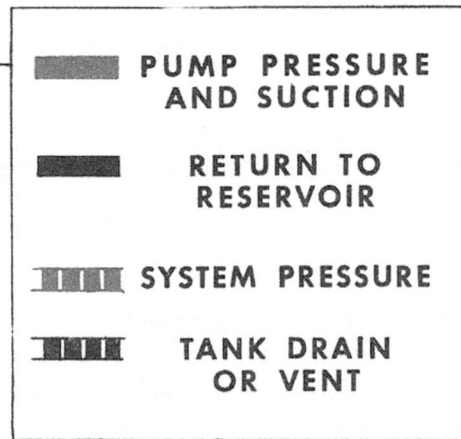

PUMP PRESSURE AND SUCTION

RETURN TO RESERVOIR

SYSTEM PRESSURE

TANK DRAIN OR VENT

You can't build up pressure with the hand hydraulic pump unless the aileron boost valve and coolant override switches are in the OFF positions.

Emergency Extension System

The emergency extension system operates from a separate reservoir and through separate lines, using the hand pump for power. **The only purpose of this system is to extend the landing gear in case of complete failure of the other two systems.**

Hydraulic Pressure Gage

A hydraulic pressure gage, on the instrument panel, shows you if the hydraulic system is working properly.

When the hydraulic system is not in use, the pressure gage registers approximately 1300 psi.

When the hydraulic system is in use, the pressure gage drops from 1300 psi to the difference in pressure remaining in the lines.

Use the hydraulic gage as a check for the correct operation of the landing gear and flaps. For example, when you lower the landing gear, the hydraulic system is put into operation. The pressure gage then drops from 1300 psi to 0. When the gage returns to its normal reading you know the landing gear is down and locked.

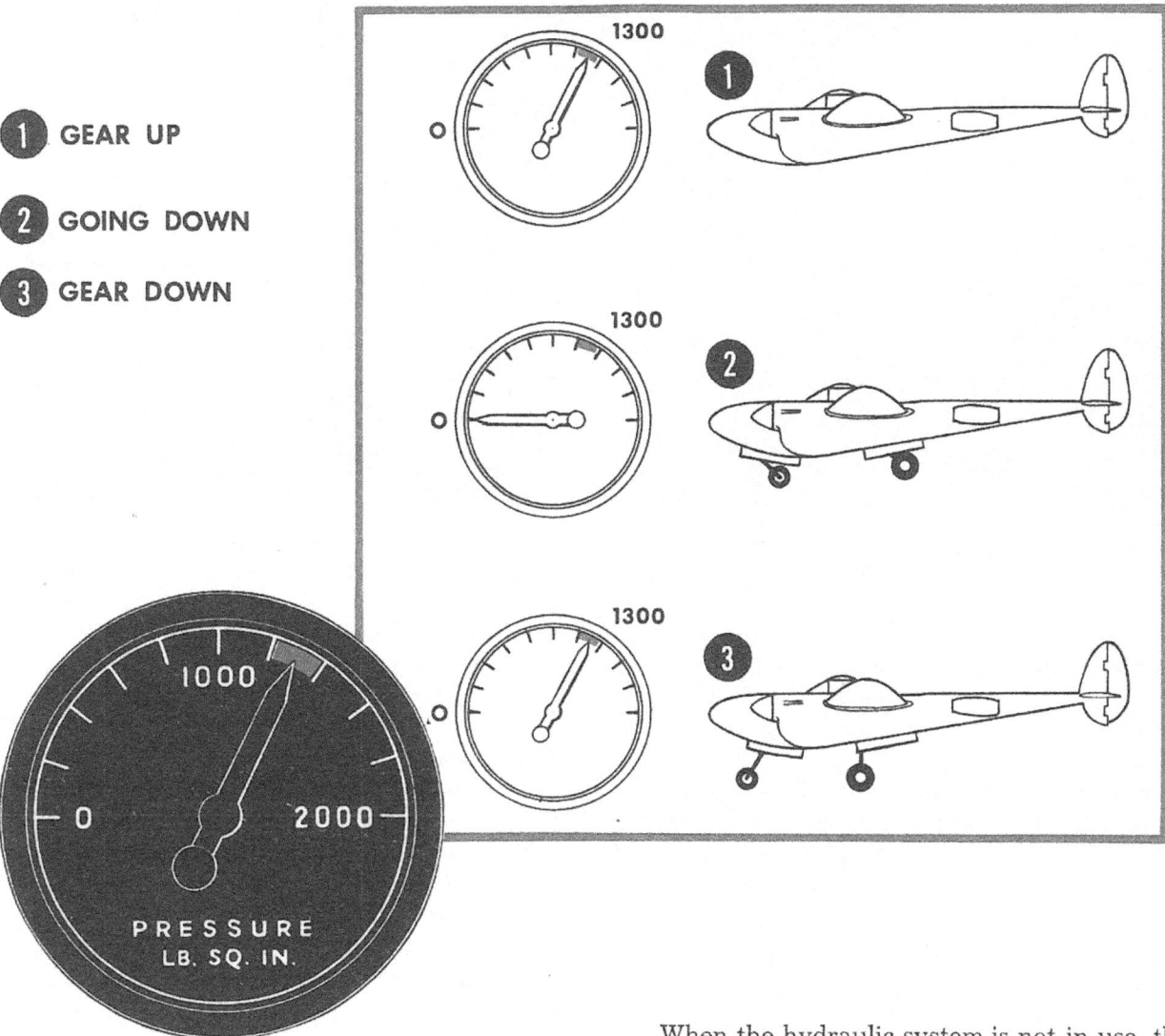

① GEAR UP

② GOING DOWN

③ GEAR DOWN

Hydraulic System Gage

P-38 series through the P-38G have, in addition to the pressure gage, a hydraulic system gage. When the hydraulic system is in use, this instrument registers the amount of pressure being used.

When the hydraulic system is not in use, the system gage registers 0. Therefore, if the gage registers a few pounds pressure when the hydraulic system is not in operation, you know that there is a leak in the hydraulic lines.

The system gage is deleted in later P-38 series that have automatic coolant flap, oil shutter, or aileron boost operation.

THE LANDING GEAR

The P-38 has a retractable tricycle landing gear. It is hydraulically operated and is controlled by a lever on the left-hand side of the cockpit. The lever has only 2 positions: UP and DOWN.

There is a safety device that prevents you from raising the landing gear lever while the main struts are compressed. This prevents retraction of the gear while the plane is on the ground.

Don't try to lift the landing gear handle while the plane is on the ground.

On P-38 series before the P-38 J-15, when the throttle is retarded to 15" Hg. or less, a warning horn sounds and a landing gear warning light on the control stand comes on if the gear is in any position other than down and locked. The P-38J and P-38L do not have a warning horn. The warning light is on the instrument panel and glows if the landing gear is not locked in either the up or down position. The P-38 series through the P-38J-10 has a position indicator on the instrument panel, for the landing gear and flaps.

The hydraulic pressure gage normally registers 1300 psi. When you put the hydraulic system into operation by raising or lowering the landing gear, the pressure drops to 0 psi. When the operation has been completed and the gear is either up or down and locked, the pressure indicated on the hydraulic gage returns to 1300 psi. Use the hydraulic pressure gage as a check that the gear is down and locked.

Shimmy Damper

The nosewheel has a shimmy damper. This device prevents the nosewheel from shimmy and vibration. You encounter severe vibration if the shimmy damper fails during taxi, takeoff run, or landing roll. Stop immediately. The nosewheel may collapse.

Operation of the Landing Gear

When you put the control handle in the UP position the gear rises.

If, after takeoff, you cannot raise the lever to the UP position, turn the emergency release knob counter-clock-wise with your left thumb. The emergency release knob is just forward of the landing gear lever.

The wheel well doors close when the landing gear reaches its retracted position. In the last quarter inch of travel, the main strut strikes a sequence valve actuating a hydraulic unit that closes the wheel doors.

You can see if the main wheel doors are closed by looking over your shoulder at the bottom section of each boom. If the gear comes up but the doors remain open, pump the stick forward. This causes the gear to press up against the sequence valve and close the doors. If that doesn't work, try lowering and raising the gear again. If the doors continue to remain open, return to your base and land. With wheel doors open or gear extended you must not exceed 175 mph.

To Retract the Landing Gear

Don't raise or lower the landing gear in a turn. The centrifugal force will put a strain on the hydraulic system.

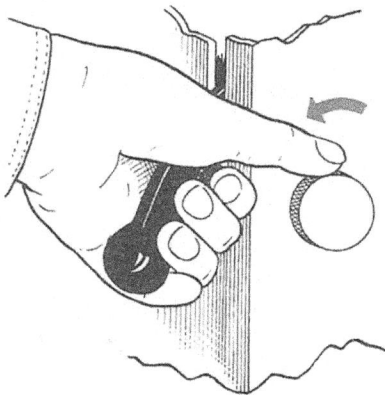

CHECK MAIN WHEEL DOORS BY LOOKING OVER SHOULDER

1. Place landing gear control handle in UP position.

2. Observe landing gear indicators. The wheels come up quite rapidly.

3. Check if wheels are up by hand hydraulic pump.

4. Check hydraulic pressure gage.

5. Look over your shoulder to see if the main wheel doors are closed.

The loud, popping noise under the seat is the pressure regulator valve, and the smoke that may come in the cockpit when the gear is raised is caused by the nosewheel rubbing on the nosewheel door. There is no cause for alarm in either case.

If the gear does not retract with the lever in the UP position, return the lever to the DOWN position and land.

To Lower Landing Gear

1. Slow the airplane to at least 175 mph.

2. Momentarily retard throttle to check operation of the warning horn and light.

Note: P-38J and P-38L do not have warning horns.

3. Place landing gear control lever in the DOWN position.

4. Watch the landing gear indicators (if installed) to see that wheels lower properly.

5. Check nosewheel position by the polished spot on the engine cowling.

6. Make sure the pressure indicator gage has returned to 1300 psi.

7. Test hand pump to make sure it resists operation.

8. Retard throttle momentarily to test warning horn (if installed) and light.

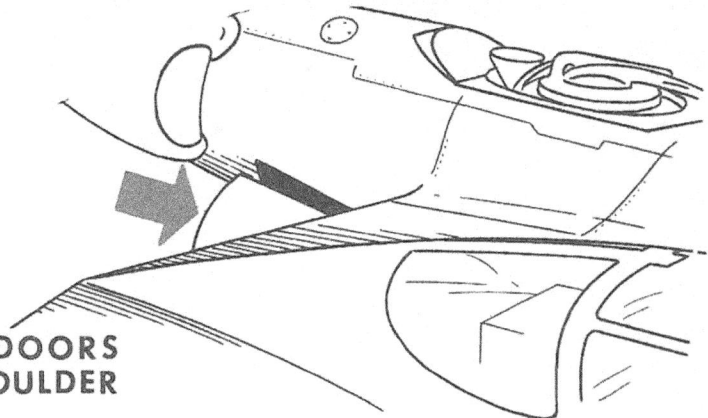

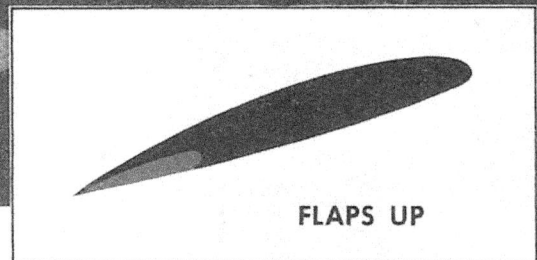

FLAPS UP

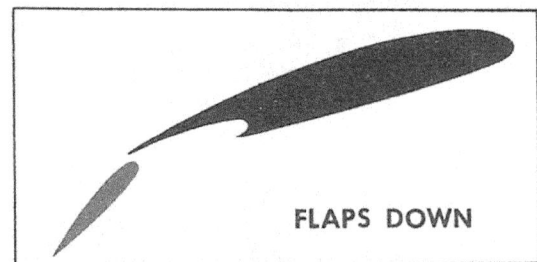

FLAPS DOWN

WING FLAPS

The P-38 has Fowler wing flaps. They slide out of the trailing edge of the wing. Using up to ½ flaps increases the wing area and provides greater lift. When the flaps are from ½ to full down, they act as air brakes.

The flaps are operated by a hydraulic motor located behind the pilot's seat. The motor makes a whining noise which, when you first hear it, may startle you.

Operation

The flap control lever is on the forward right-hand side of the cockpit. The UP, DOWN, and MANEU (Maneuver) positions control the direction of flap movement. The CLOSED position enables you to stop the motion and lock the flaps in any desired intermediate position.

A flap position indicator on the instrument panel shows you the position of the flaps. Some later series indicate the flap position by a small, pop-up lever on the trailing edge of the left wing just inside of the boom. This indicator projects above the wing whenever the flaps are not full up.

To lower the flaps, move the control lever to the DOWN position. The lever will not go to the DOWN position until the trigger on the lever is lifted through the notch forward of the CLOSED position. Return the lever to the CLOSED position when the flap indicator shows the desired amount of flaps.

To raise the flaps, move the control lever to UP.

When not in use, leave the control lever in the CLOSED position.

Don't lower full flaps at airspeeds over 150 mph.

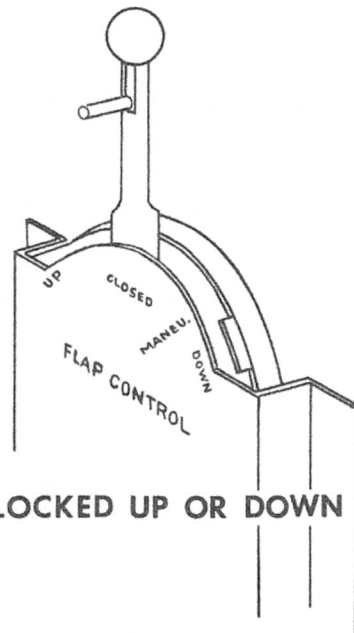

FLAPS LOCKED UP OR DOWN

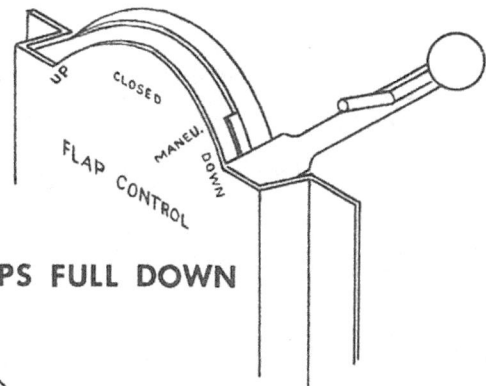

FLAPS FULL DOWN

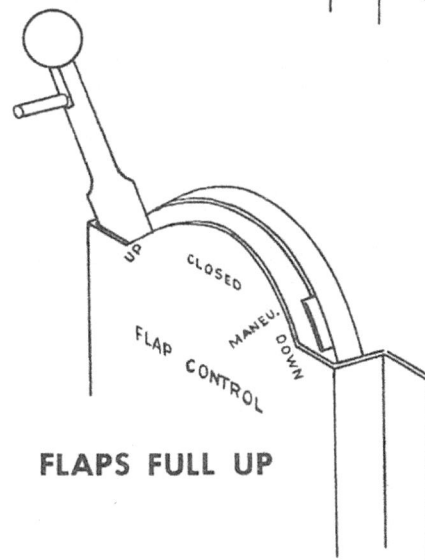

FLAPS FULL UP

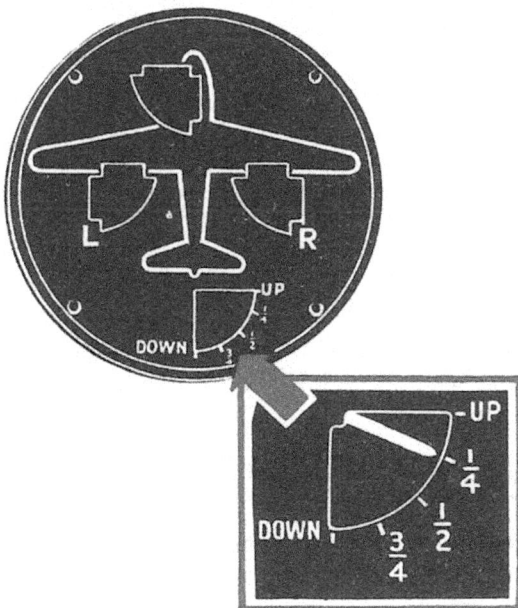

Maneuver Flaps

Pull the flap control lever back to the MANEU position without lifting the trigger through the notch, and you get maneuver flaps (approximately ½ flaps). One-half flaps increases lift and lowers the stalling speed. This provides the P-38 with greater maneuverability.

You can lower maneuver flaps, also known as combat flaps, at airspeeds up to 250 mph IAS.

Dive Flaps

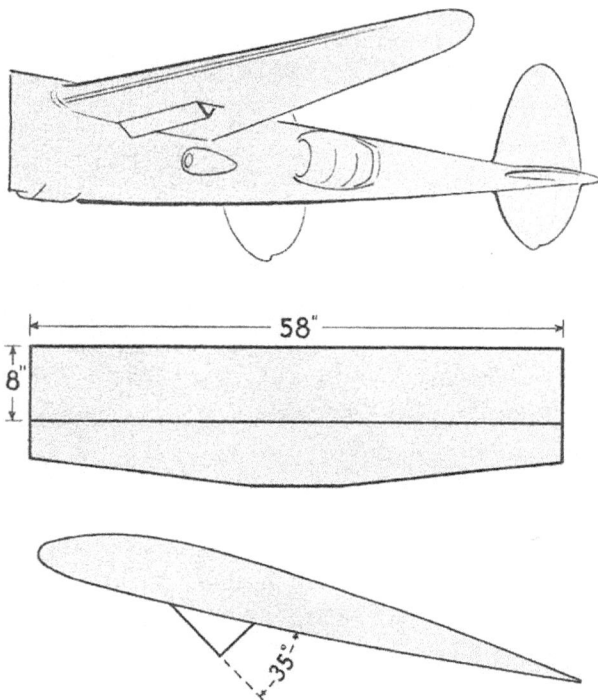

The P-38L and later P-38J series have dive flaps. They are just behind and below the leading edge of the wing, outboard of the engine nacelles. They are approximately 58 inches long and 8 inches wide.

The flaps are electrically controlled by a toggle switch on the left-hand side of the control wheel.

The dive flaps are either up or down. There is no intermediate position. They extend or retract within 2 seconds and have a 35° angle when in the down position.

Aileron Boost

Another new addition is the aileron boost. It is exactly what its name implies. It is hydraulically operated and triples the rate of roll. The aileron boost control is on the right side of the cockpit under the flap handle. It has 2 positions: ON and OFF.

This makes the P-38L and later P-38J's extremely maneuverable at any speed.

Aileron boost must be ON **all the time** except for the following conditions:
Single engine landing.
Hydraulic trouble.

Note: The ailerons ride approximately 1 inch higher with boost OFF. This change in trim is normal.

Important!

Do not turn aileron boost ON during flight. If you have started a flight with aileron boost OFF, or have turned it OFF for emergency operation, don't turn it ON again until you have landed.

ELECTRICAL SYSTEM

The electrical system consists of a 100-ampere generator mounted on the left engine, a voltage regulator, a reverse current relay, a battery located in the left boom (in the nose compartment of the F-5), a battery switch, generator switch, ammeter, and voltmeter. Some P-38's have two generators, one mounted on each engine.

The generator is the primary source of power for all electrical equipment. Be sure the generator is on at all times.

The voltage regulator keeps the generator voltage constant. A constant voltage of 28.5 volts is necessary to operate the electrical equipment and to keep the battery charged.

The reverse current relay automatically disconnects the generator from the main circuit when the engine stops or the generator fails.

The battery is a small power reserve to supply extra power for momentary peak loads. Don't use it as a primary source of power. Be sure the generator is on and working properly.

The battery switch connects and disconnects the battery from the main circuit.

The generator switch connects and disconnects the generator from the main circuit.

The ammeter indicates the charging current to the battery and electrical system. Normal reading is not to exceed 50 amps.

The voltmeter indicates the voltage output of the generator. Any deviation greater than +2 or —2 volts from a reading of 28.5 volts on the voltmeter is reason to check condition of voltage regulator or generator.

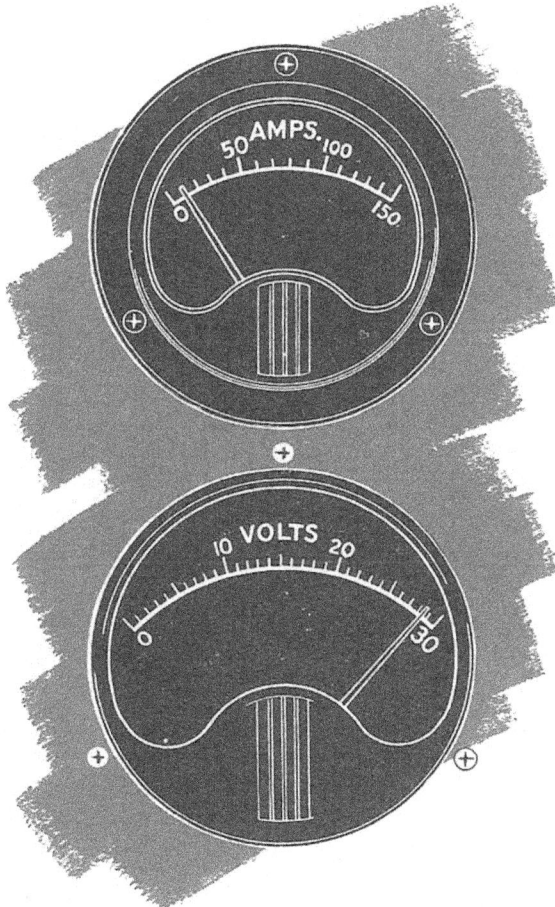

Inverter

An inverter supplies current to specific instruments. The inverter switch is located either on the main switch box or directly under the flap control handle. The inverter must be on. Many P-38's up to and including the P-38H have an inverter warning light installed. When the light is on, the inverter is not in operation.

The inverter on the P-38J and P-38L operates only the remote compass. There is no warning light. Turn on the inverter by a switch on the main switch box labeled COMPASS; ON-OFF.

Circuit Breakers and Fuses

The circuit breakers mounted along the right side of the cockpit on later series P-38's act as fuses and automatically break the circuit when an overload occurs. They replace the fuses in the nose wheel well in earlier series. Reset a circuit breaker by allowing a short interval for cooling and then pushing the button. Unlike the propeller circuit breakers, these buttons do not pop out and it is not possible to tell by looking at them whether or not a circuit breaker is open.

COMMUNICATIONS

Most P-38's have a VHF command radio, an auxiliary battery radio, and an IFF (Identification, friend or foe) set.

VHF Command Set (SCR-522-A Radio)

The transmitter and receiver operate on four pre-tuned channels. It is a powerful radio, having a range of more than 150 miles. It transmits and receives on direct line of sight. If there are any obstructions between you and the airplane or station you are calling, your transmission will not be received.

The control box is on the right-hand side of the cockpit. There are 5 push buttons on the control box. The first one is the OFF button. The others, A, B, C, and D, turn on the transmitter and receiver and select the frequency.

The control box also has a lever that varies the intensity of the channel indicator lights, and a T-R-REM switch. When the T-R-REM switch is set to T, you can transmit but not receive. When it is set to R, you can receive but not transmit. When it is set to the REM position, you have remote operation and can transmit and receive. The T and R positions are for emergency operation. The T-R-REM switch is usually wired to the REM position.

With the T-R-REM switch in the REM position, you can transmit by pressing the microphone button on the control wheel.

You use a throat microphone or an oxygen mask microphone with this radio. Be sure the jacks are plugged in properly and you have checked all your equipment.

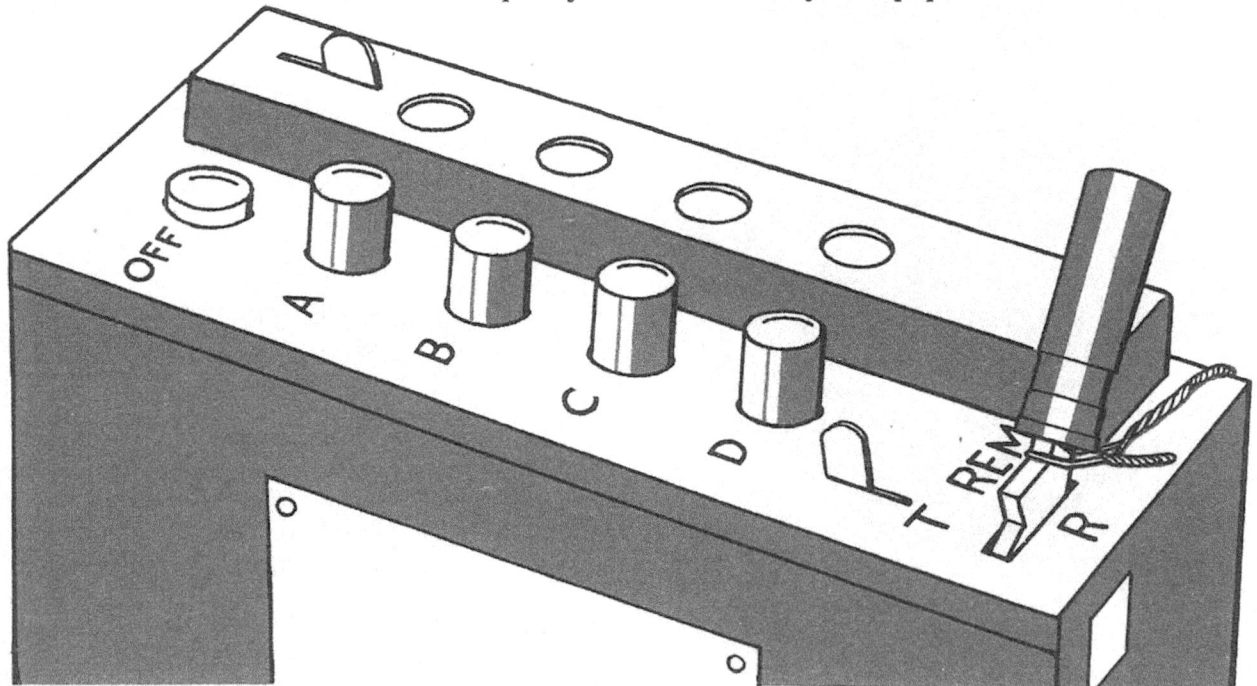

Operation of the Radio

1. Airplane battery switch ON.
2. Make sure your headset and microphone are plugged in jacks.
3. Control switch in REM position.
4. Press A, B, C, or D channel button as desired.
5. To transmit, press microphone button in center of control wheel (on hand grip on P-38J and P-38L). Speak slowly and clearly.

Caution

Voltages developed by transmitters are sufficiently high to cause severe burns or death. Before you transmit on the ground, be sure no one is close to the antenna.

6. To turn radio equipment off, press OFF button.

Auxiliary Radio

P-38 models with VHF radios also have an auxiliary range receiver. It covers frequencies from 200 to 400 kilocycles.

This auxiliary set is on the right side of the cockpit below VHF radio switch box.

To operate:

1. Turn the set on. Switch is on the face of the set.
2. Turn volume up until you hear the background noise.
3. Tune to desired frequency.

IFF

Identification Friend or Foe

SCR-695 Radio

The receiver for the IFF is in the right boom, between the coolant radiators and the baggage compartment.

The control box is on the left-hand side of the cockpit. It contains an ON-OFF switch and a 6-position selector switch. To turn the IFF equipment on, place the ON-OFF switch in the ON position. Your communications officer will instruct you concerning the correct selector switch settings.

Destructor Unit

The IFF equipment is secret. If you make a forced landing in enemy territory, destroy the IFF. Two push button switches are located directly below the control box. They are operated by current from the airplane electrical system. When you press both buttons simultaneously, you destroy the receiver in the tail boom. **The receiver is destroyed but nothing else!**

If you bail out or make a crash landing, the IFF will automatically be destroyed when the airplane hits the ground. The destructor unit is set to go off automatically when 6 G's or more are applied.

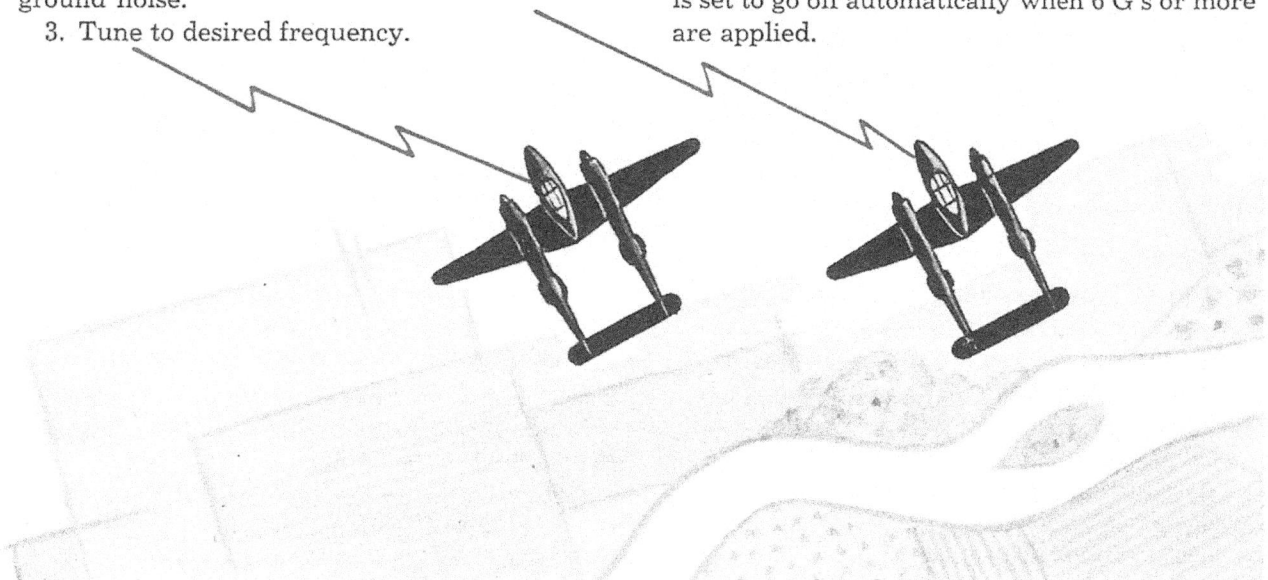

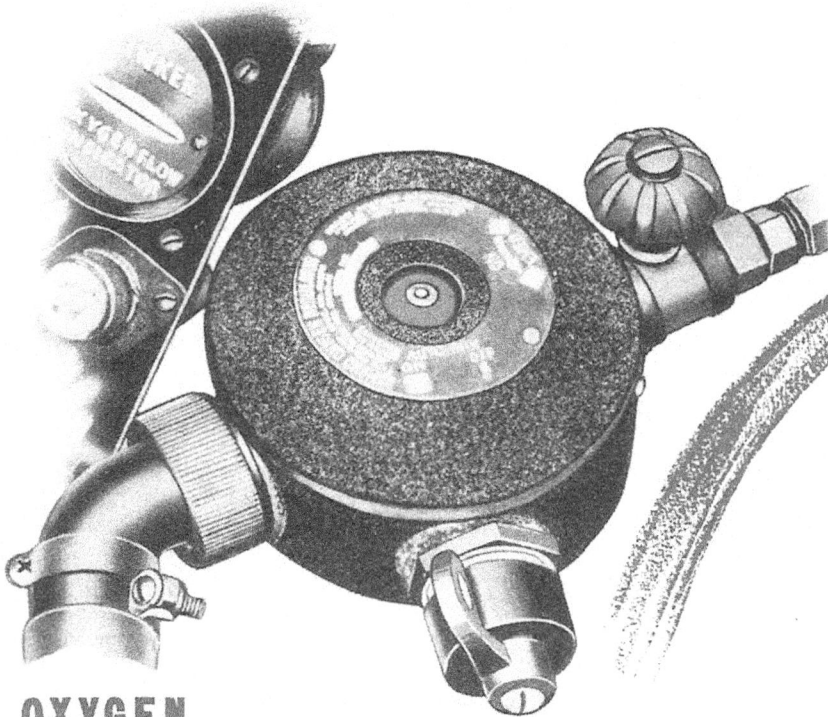

OXYGEN

You have a low pressure, demand type, oxygen system. It is important that you understand the oxygen system and the use of the oxygen mask. Check with your personal equipment officer and flight surgeon concerning the use and fit of your mask. Know the symptoms and danger of anoxia.

The Mask

You have either an A-10 or A-14 demand type oxygen mask. Both work perfectly on this system. Fit the mask snugly. Check it for leaks by holding your thumb over the end of the hose and breathing in gently. If you find it difficult to breathe, it is a good fit. Wash your mask after each use and inspect it regularly.

The System

There are 3 oxygen bottles in your airplane; 2 in the left boom and 1 in the right. The bottles are filled to a pressure of 400 to 450 psi. This gives you more than a 6-hour supply of oxygen at 30,000 feet. A pressure gage on the left side of the cockpit near the landing gear control handle indicates the amount of pressure in the system. A supply warning light indicates when the pressure drops below 100 psi.

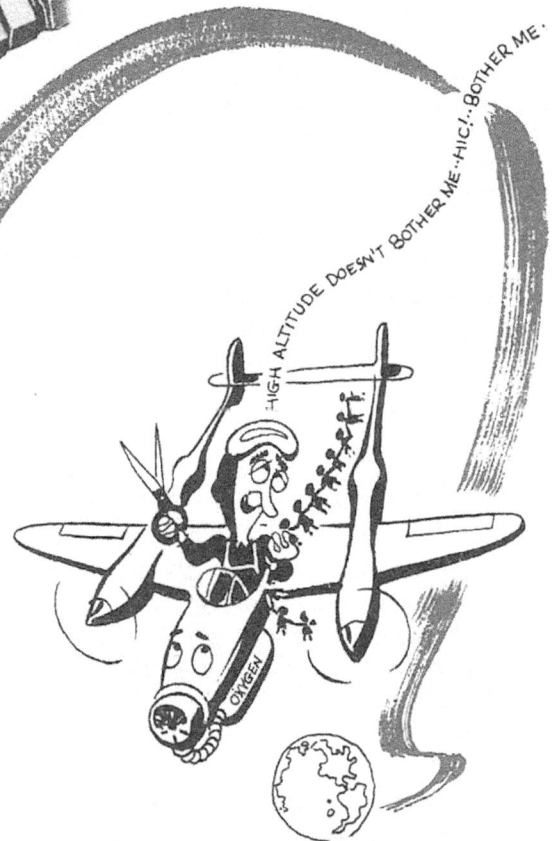

There is an oxygen regulator with an auto-mix lever. The lever has 2 positions: ON and OFF. When the lever is in the ON position, the regulator automatically mixes air with the oxygen to give you the supply you demand at any altitude. With the auto-mix lever in the OFF position, you receive pure oxygen every time you inhale.

A small knob for emergency use is on the regulator. By turning the knob counter-clockwise you convert the demand system to free flow. This allows oxygen to flow at a steady rate whether you inhale or not. **Use it only if the demand system fails.**

A flow meter on the regulator indicates that the system is operating properly. It is a blinker that opens and closes as you breathe.

How to Use the Oxygen System

Plan to use oxygen on all flights above 12,000 feet. Breathe normally whenever you use oxygen. Only a certain amount of oxygen can be absorbed. When the blood becomes saturated, the rest is wasted.

1. After you are in the cockpit, connect your mask to the tube leading to the regulator. Be sure the connection is a snug fit. Test it and see that it doesn't separate easily.

2. Clip the mask tube to your clothing, allowing for head movement without pulling the mask or tube loose.

3. Turn the auto-mix lever ON and be sure the emergency knob is OFF.

4. Constantly check the pressure and flow during flight.

5. Turn the auto-mix lever OFF at 30,000 feet and over.

At 30,000 feet you receive pure oxygen with the auto-mix lever either ON or OFF. But with it OFF you are abruptly informed when the supply is exhausted because you can't get another breath through the mask. It feels as if someone has put a finger over the end of the tube. This is your warning to get down to a safe altitude where oxygen isn't needed. If you leave the auto-mix lever in the ON position and the supply is exhausted, you would continue to breathe as before, but the regulator would be supplying nothing but cockpit air. After a few minutes of such breathing you would be overcome by anoxia.

Emergency System

If the supply warning light comes on, immediately descend to below 12,000 feet. A leak in the system can cause a very rapid loss of oxygen.

If the flow meter (blinker) stops but you still have oxygen pressure, immediately check your mask for fit and the tube connection. If this doesn't start the flow meter, the demand part of the system has probably failed. Turn the emergency knob to ON. The oxygen supply under these conditions depletes rapidly, so start your descent to a safe altitude.

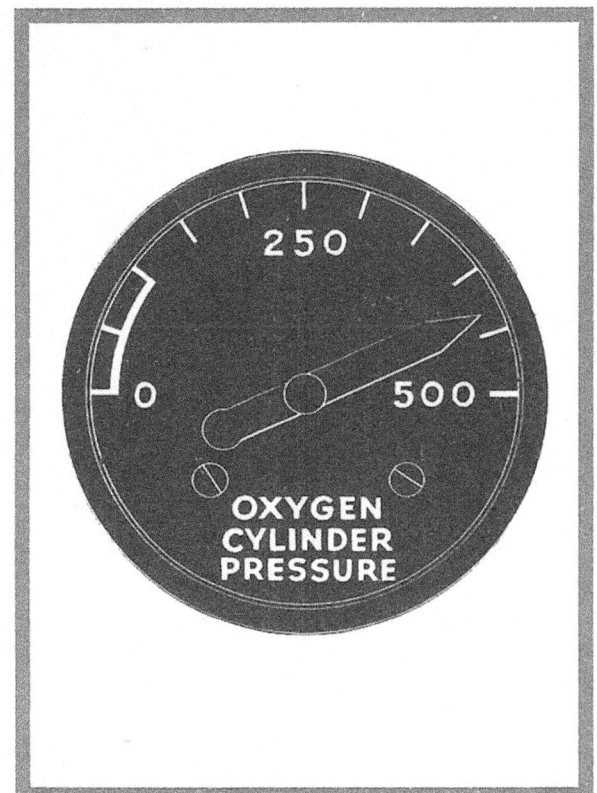

ARMAMENT

You have four .50-cal. machine guns and one
20-mm. cannon. Three hundred to 500 rounds
are carried for each machine gun and up to
150 rounds for the cannon.

To fire the guns, you press trigger buttons
on the right side of the control wheel. You fire
the 4 machine guns when you press the trigger
on the rear of the wheel with your index finger.
You fire the cannon by pressing the trigger on
the front or top of the wheel with your thumb.
A small motion picture camera is synchronized
with the guns.

RESTRICTED

Operation of the Machine Guns

Before takeoff, check to see that your machine guns and cannon have been charged. If your airplane isn't equipped with charging facilities, check with the crew chief. Most P-38's up to the J series have the machine gun charger in the cockpit.

To charge the machine guns:

1. Pull the selector knob out and turn it to the gun to be charged.

2. Pull the charging handle all the way back until it clicks and then push it forward.

3. Strike the selector knob with the heel of your hand.

Note: This operation is absolutely necessary to complete charging of the gun.

Never move the selector knob unless the charging handle is in the full forward position.

4. Charge the other 3 guns in the same manner.

Your armorer will tell you the position of the first shell. Sometimes it is necessary to charge the machine guns twice to insert the first live shell.

The machine guns do not have to be recharged after firing except in the case of a jam.

To Fire the Machine Guns

1. Turn armament master switch and machine gun switch ON.

If the airplane has a camera-combat switch, set it to COMBAT. The camera-combat switch is on the control column switch box and replaces all other armament switches.

2. Press the machine gun button with your index finger.

Turn gun heat ON whenever the outside air temperature is below freezing.

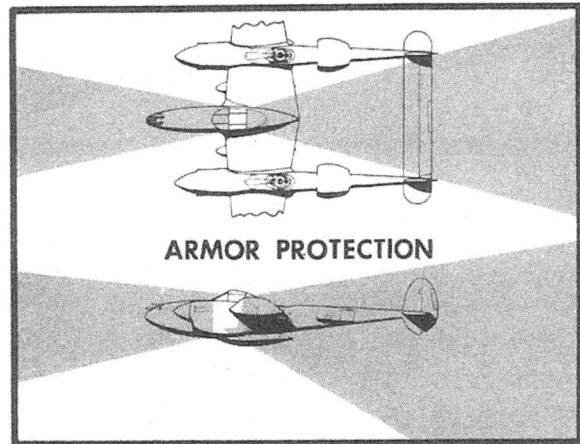

ARMOR PROTECTION

Operation of the 20-mm. Cannon

The cannon is charged by the ground crew. There is no way to remedy a cannon jam while in flight.

To Fire the Cannon

1. Armament switch on COMBAT.
2. Press cannon button.

Before you land, be sure you have turned all gun switches OFF.

The Optical Gunsight

Turn the airplane master switch and the gunsight rheostat ON. Adjust the brilliancy of the reflection as desired.

Some sights have a sunshade. The sunshade is kept in a box over the fuel cocks. You can install it on top of the sight reflector when necessary.

The Gun Camera

The camera operates automatically when either the cannon or machine guns are fired. If you want to use only the camera without firing the guns, set the armament switch to CAMERA and press either the machine gun or cannon button.

The camera is in the nose and slightly below the guns. The camera on the P-38L and later P-38J series is under the left wing in the drop tank shackle-housing.

Heating

Cockpit heat and warm air to defrost the windshield are supplied by an intensifier tube connected to the right engine exhaust. The cockpit heat control is on the right windshield support.

There is a heat outlet for your feet. Open and close it by the control on the floor under your right foot.

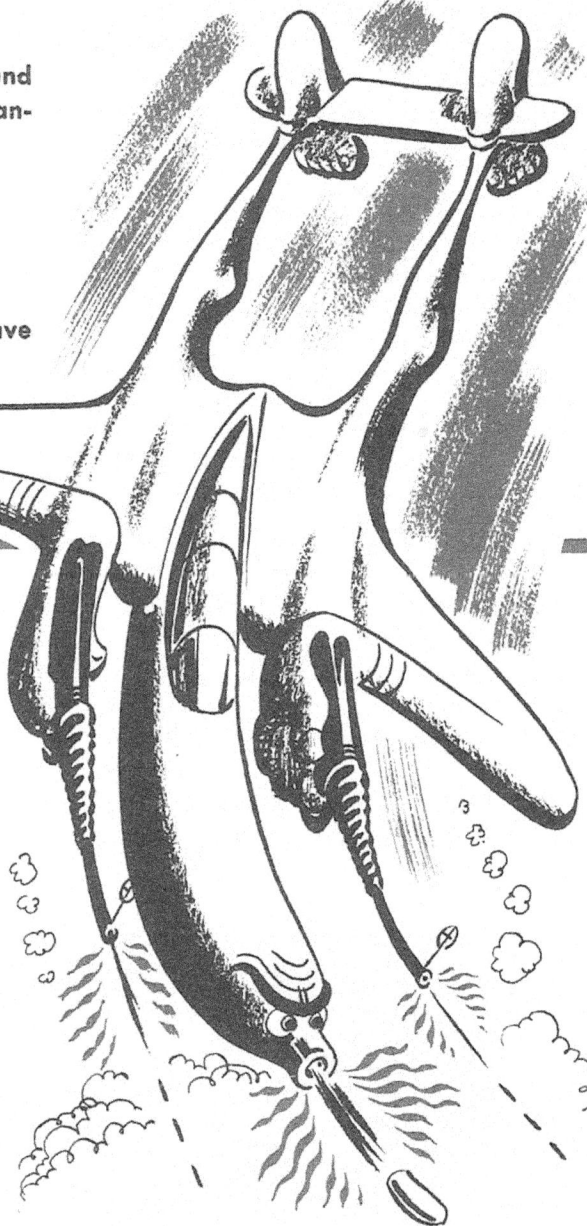

Armament and camera compartment heat is supplied by an intensifier tube connected to the left engine exhaust. The control is on the left windshield support on early airplanes. On later airplanes the left engine heat has been diverted to the cockpit and the armament is electrically heated. Electric gun heaters are turned on by a switch on the main switch box.

LIGHTING EQUIPMENT

Landing Light

P-38 Series Through P-38J-15

A retractable landing light is under the left wing. You control it by a 3-position toggle switch on the main switch box. Some P-38 series have two landing lights.

With the landing light switch in the ON position, the light extends and turns on. Place the switch in the RETRACT position to retract the light and turn it off. Leave the landing light switch in the OFF position when not in use.

Extend the landing light at an airspeed of not more than 140 mph.

P-38J-20 Through P-38L

The landing light is in the leading edge of the left wing and is turned on or off by a 2-position toggle switch.

Aileron Nibble

When the landing light is extended, it disturbs the airflow over the aileron. This causes an aileron nibble which you feel in the control column. The vibration increases with an increase of airspeed. Don't be alarmed. There is no change in flight characteristics. To stop the vibration, retract the light or reduce speed.

Recognition Lights

Three recognition lights, red, green, and amber, are on the underside of the gondola. On some airplanes a white recognition light is behind the pilot's compartment on the radio equipment. These lights are used as an aid in night formation flying, for signals, and, in combat, for identification.

The four recognition lights are controlled by switches on a control box on the righthand side of the cockpit. The control box is labeled LITE. The switches have 3 positions: OFF, STEADY, and KEY. To turn the lights on, place the switches in the STEADY position. When the switches are in the KEY position, you must press the button on the top of the control box to turn the lights on. Use the KEY position for code or flash signaling.

Do not operate the colored recognition lights for more than 10 seconds on the ground. The heat of the lights will burn through the plastic lenses.

Position Lights

You control them by switches on the main switch box. BRIGHT, DIM, and OFF positions are provided.

Cockpit Lights

You control them by a rheostat on the main switch box and a switch on the lights themselves.

Fluorescent Instrument Lights

They are mounted behind the control column and turned on by a switch on the main switch box. Regulate the light intensity by twisting the ends of the lighting unit.

Spotlight

It is normally on the left windshield support. An alternate position is provided over the fuel tank selector valves. The spotlight switch is on the light, and you can focus the beam by sliding the screw head forward and aft in its slot.

RETRACTABLE LADDER

The P-38 has a retractable ladder on the rear of the gondola. To lower the ladder:

1. Push the uplock release.
2. Raise the handle to a vertical position.
3. Force the handle down until the ladder locks in the down position.

To Retract the Ladder

1. Push the downlock release.
2. Pull the handle straight up until the ladder stows in place.
3. Swing the handle forward until it is flush with the gondola contour and press firmly into place.

Always use the retractable ladder to get up on the wing. On later airplanes, a flush hinged handhold is built into the left side of the fuselage.

SECTION 3 CHECKS AND FLIGHT

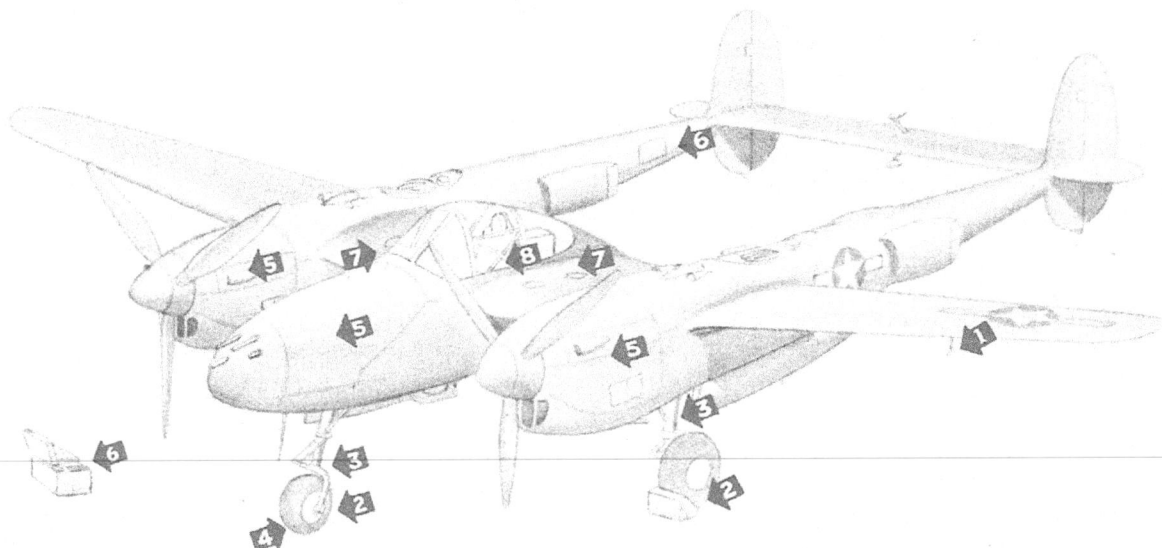

VISUAL INSPECTION CHECK

Make a complete visual inspection of the airplane.

Try to be out to your airplane at least a half-hour before scheduled takeoff time. This enables you to give the airplane a thorough check and discuss with your crew chief what repairs or changes have been made.

Check the following

1. Pitot cover removed.
2. Wheels blocked and tires properly inflated.
3. Oleo struts—main wheels extended 2½ to 4 inches. Nosewheel extended 4 to 6 inches.
4. Direction of nosewheel.
5. Cowling fasteners secure.
6. Obstructions close to airplane; tool kits, other aircraft, etc.
Tip: Inspect the baggage compartment in the right boom before each flight. Too much weight in the baggage compartment can cause a tail-heavy condition and put your plane out of trim.
Note: The P-38 with full complement of guns, ammunition, and fuel (including drop tanks or

bombs) has a center of gravity within the permissible range.

7. Fuel tanks full and caps secure.

To get up on the wing, always use the retractable ladder on the rear of the gondola.

8. Check clearance between dive fillets and windows. Maximum allowable is 3/16 inch. If a plastic seal strip is on the lower part of the window, the dive fillet is flush with the strip.

Tip: The weight of a few men on the horizontal stabilizer will lift the nosewheel off the ground and straighten it.

Hey! I'm okeh now!

58   RESTRICTED

PREFLIGHT CHECK

Spend as much time as you can with your ground crew. Learn how they perform a preflight inspection, and become confident that you can do it yourself. There may be occasions when you will land at a strange base and find there are no mechanics who know how to preflight your P-38. You will have to perform the preflight before you can take off. Ask your crew chief to show you how to make this check:

1. Bleed the turbo-supercharger balance lines to insure proper performance of the superchargers. The petcocks for this operation are in the main wheel wells. Screw petcock in and allow water to drain. Then screw it out again and re-safety.

2. Drain the fuel strainers, which are under the center portion of the gondola. Remove the recognition light panel and drain about a pint of gasoline from the 4 petcocks. Then close and re-safety.

3. Check the supercharger wastegate for freedom of movement. It's behind the turbo-wheel.

4. Examine turbo wheel for elongated buckets and cracks.

5. Check to be sure you have sufficient fuel, oil, coolant, and hydraulic fluid. The oil tanks are outboard of the engine nacelles near the leading edge of the wing. Fill to approximately 4 inches from the top. The hydraulic fluid reservoir is on top of the gondola and behind the canopy. Fill to the strainer and turn purolator filter two revolutions.

6. Pull the propellers through at least 3 times.

7. Make a complete visual check of the airplane.

8. Start the left engine and check the hydraulic pump operation by lowering and raising the flaps. Note the time the operation takes.

9. Start the right engine and check right hydraulic pump by lowering and raising flaps. This operation with both engines running requires approximately half the time it takes with one engine.

10. Test feather switches. Do not allow the propellers to feather completely.

11. Test all warning lights.

So sorry, Kaptain, but ve iss not familiar wis your~~vot you call id~~ P-sirty-edd?~~you vill yoursselluf hass to check her!

Fuel, Oil, Coolant, and Hydraulic Specifications

Fuel

Specification AN-VV-F-781 (Amendment No. 5 or better), AN-F-28, or AN-F-29 (Grade 100 Fuel.). AN-F-26 (Grade 91 Fuel; refer to T. O. No. 02-1-38 and 02-5A-66A).

Engine Oil

Specification AN-VV-O-446, Grade 1120. For cold weather operation, Grade 1100A.

Supercharger Oil

Specification AN-VV-446, Grade 1065.

Coolant

Specification AN-E-2 (Ethylene Glycol—inhibited with NaMBT).

Hydraulic Fluid

Specification AN-VV-O-366.

COCKPIT CHECK

1. Check the Form 1A. Discuss it thoroughly with your crew chief.

2. Secure parachute, shoulder harness, and safety belt. Adjust the seat by lifting the small lever on the right side of the seat. After you have adjusted the seat and released the lever, check to make sure the seat is firmly locked in the new position.

Important: Don't wear the shoulder harness if you can't reach all the controls when it is on and unlocked, except in preparation for an emergency landing.

Notice to pilots with short legs: Use cushions to place you well forward in the cockpit. This will give you full rudder control.

3. Connect head set and adjust throat mike; look to see that mike jack is in place.

4. Close the canopy and make sure it is locked.

Check to be sure that both catches of the canopy overlap and that the rear pins are securely in position.

5. Check for free movement of the flight controls to the extremities of their operating range.

Adjust rudder pedals for correct leg length by means of the spring-loaded levers on the pedals.

6. See that control lock is in place.

7. Adjust trim tabs to proper setting—rudder and aileron neutral elevator 3° back.

8. Fuel selectors to RESERVE. (Set fuel selectors by click and feel.)

9. Crossfeed and booster pump OFF.

10. Turn bomb selector switches ON and arming switch to SAFE.

This is a must when carrying drop tanks or bombs so that you can get rid of them quickly if an engine fails on takeoff.

11. Crack throttles.

12. Propeller control governors full forward in takeoff position.

13. Propeller selector switches in AUTOMATIC.

14. Mixture controls in IDLE CUT-OFF.

15. Carburetor air filter lever as required.

On series previous to the P-38J this position on engine control stand has 2 coolant shutter control levers. Place them full forward to OPEN.

16. Propeller circuit breakers ON.

17. Propeller feathering switches in NORMAL.

18. Set clock and altimeter.

19. Check to see that oxygen pressure is 400 to 450 psi.

20. Be sure all gun switches are OFF.

21. Flap handle in UP position.

22. Aileron boost ON.

23. Radio OFF.

24. Test auxiliary hand hydraulic pump.

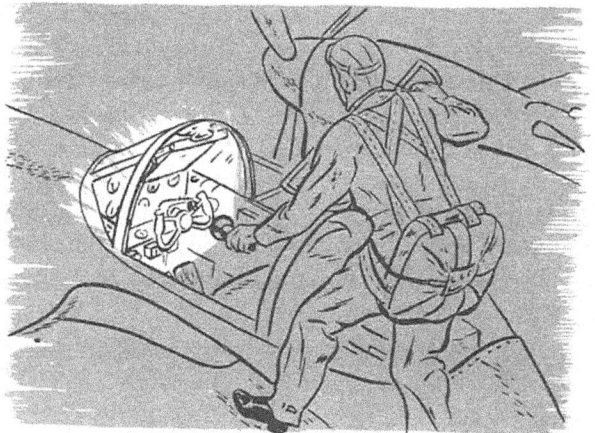

Special Check for Night Flying

Test operation of:

1. Landing lights (not more than 5 seconds with engines not running).

2. Recognition lights (not more than 10 seconds on the ground).

3. Cockpit lights.

4. Fluorescent lights.

5. Position lights.

6. Spotlight.

There are no engine fire extinguishers in the P-38. Reduce the possibility of fire by adhering strictly to the following information concerning the use of the mixture controls.

Important: If a fire occurs while you're starting an engine, immediately return the mixture control to IDLE CUT-OFF. Then turn fuel selector valve, fuel booster pump, and ignition OFF.

There is one primer for both engines. Push the handle down to unlock it, and turn it 90° toward the engine you want to prime. Be primer-conscious. **Under-prime rather than over-prime.** Too much prime floods the engines and creates a fire hazard.

If your battery power is not sufficient for starting, use the inertia hand crank or an external energizer.

Be sure you are ready to go before starting the engines, for they overheat rapidly. Always start the left engine first.

1. Prime 2 to 4 strokes.

Cold engines require more prime than warm engines.

2. Battery and ignition switches ON.

Use a battery cart if available. If you do use one, do not turn battery switch on until after you've started the engines.

3. Turn generator switch(es) ON.

Exception: Army depots equipped many P-38's with 2 generators. These are not the same as factory modifications with 2 generators. In this case, turn on only 1 generator for starting and during flight.

4. Turn booster pump ON.
5. ENERGIZE engine.
6. Turn booster pump OFF.
7. ENGAGE the starter. Hold it until the engine definitely fires.
8. When the engine definitely fires, advance the mixture control to AUTO RICH.

Important: If the engine dies, immediately return the mixture control to IDLE CUT-OFF.

9. Idle the engine at 1000 rpm—above vibration and fouling point.

Now, start the right engine in the same manner.

Stop the engines if the oil pressure does not register within 30 seconds.

After Both Engines Are Running Smoothly:

1. Turn the radio ON and tune to proper frequency.

2. Inverter switch (or compass switch on switch box) ON.

3. Coolant and oil shutters as required for warm-up. (In AUTOMATIC position on P-38H and P-38J.)

4. Intercooler shutters OPEN (if installed.)

5. Check gunsight light.

6. Push button to test turbo or fuel warning light.

7. Check fuel quantity gages.

Engine Warm-up

The engine warm-up is comparable to the few turns you make around the track before you really start to run.

Don't exceed 1400 rpm until minimum temperatures and pressures have been reached—oil temperature at least 40°C, and oil pressure between the red lines (approximately 75 psi).

Oil pressure may be high if the engines are cold and low if the engines are hot. Don't leave the line until the oil pressure is within the red line limits.

Other temperature and pressures are:

1. Coolant temperature—at least 85°C.

2. Fuel pressure—between 16 and 18 psi.

3. Hydraulic pressure — between 1100 and 1400 psi.

After the above minimum temperatures and pressures are reached, place the coolant and oil shutters in the full open position. This helps to prevent the engines from over-heating.

NOW YOU ARE READY TO TAXI

TAXI TECHNIQUE

The airplane taxis easily. There is no danger of a nose-over or a groundloop if you find you must turn sharply or apply full brakes. You have unobstructed vision because the airplane is in a level attitude and you are surrounded by plexiglas.

Remember
THERE IS NO EXCUSE FOR A TAXI ACCIDENT

TAXI PROCEDURE

Be sure your crew chief and all other members of the ground crew are clear of the airplane before you start to taxi. Your job is to kill the enemy, not your friends.

1. Establish proper radio contact before leaving the line.

(Have forward motion before turning.)
2. Look out both sides and in front.
3. Taxi slowly.
(Always keep your brakes pumped up.)
4. Brake intermittently, not continuously. Don't ride the brakes.
5. Turn slow and wide. A sharp turn causes stress on the nosewheel.
6. Keep your hand on the throttles and your feet on the rudder pedals at all times.
7. Stay on the taxi strip. The P-38 is a heavy airplane and will bog down in the soft earth—an easy way to snap a nosewheel.
8. Stop at a 45° angle to the runway so that you have good rear and forward vision.
9. Be sure it is clear behind you before you run up the engines. Be both a pilot and a gentleman.
10. Test brakes in taxiing out. If either or both brakes are weak, return to the line.

HOW TO HOLD AND USE TOE BRAKES

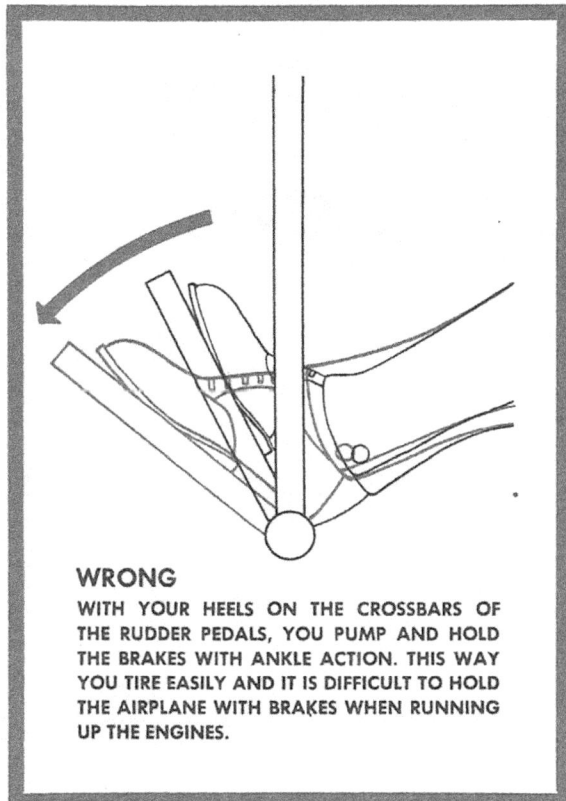

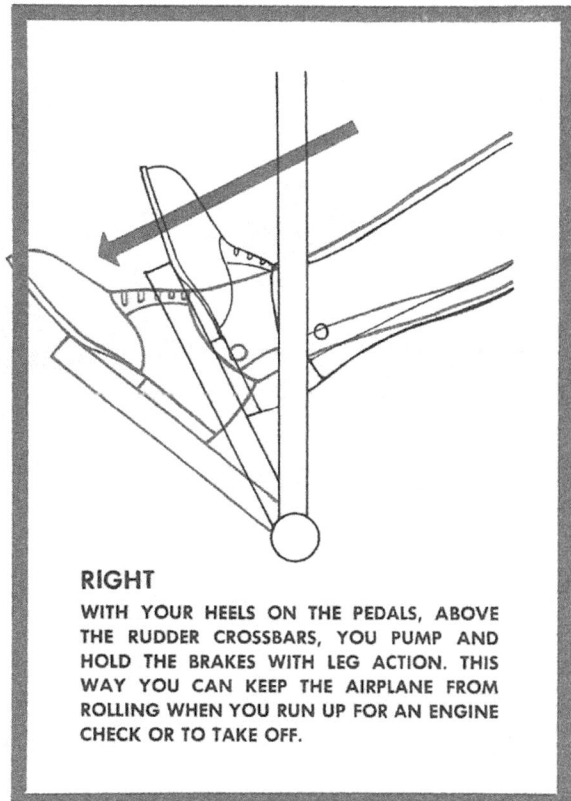

WRONG
WITH YOUR HEELS ON THE CROSSBARS OF THE RUDDER PEDALS, YOU PUMP AND HOLD THE BRAKES WITH ANKLE ACTION. THIS WAY YOU TIRE EASILY AND IT IS DIFFICULT TO HOLD THE AIRPLANE WITH BRAKES WHEN RUNNING UP THE ENGINES.

RIGHT
WITH YOUR HEELS ON THE PEDALS, ABOVE THE RUDDER CROSSBARS, YOU PUMP AND HOLD THE BRAKES WITH LEG ACTION. THIS WAY YOU CAN KEEP THE AIRPLANE FROM ROLLING WHEN YOU RUN UP FOR AN ENGINE CHECK OR TO TAKE OFF.

BEFORE TAKEOFF

This is the time when you can find out what you want to know about your airplane. Don't be in a hurry to take off. A little extra time before takeoff can save you a lot of trouble after you are in the air.

Here is the check you make before takeoff. Follow it closely!

1. Safety belt locked. Shoulder harness on and unlocked.
2. Canopy locked and side windows closed with ratchets ON.
3. Rudder and aileron tabs at 0.
4. Elevator trim tab 0° to 3° back (this relieves pressure on control column).
5. Fuel selectors on RESERVE.
6. Electric fuel booster pumps ON.
7. Drop tank selector switches ON and arming switch SAFE.
8. Propeller governor controls full forward.
9. Propeller selector switches AUTOMATIC.
10. Tighten friction control.
11. Mixture control AUTO RICH.
12. Generator switch (es) ON.
13. Oil and coolant shutters AUTOMATIC.
14. Intercooler flaps OPEN. (If installed.)
15. Dive flaps UP.
16. Wing flaps up and control handle in NEUTRAL.
17. Aileron boost ON.

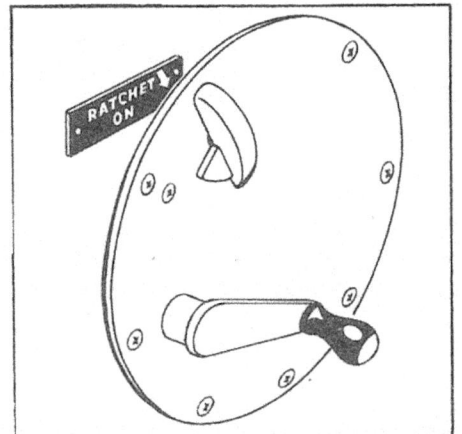

Tip

The windows slide down if ratchets are not ON. If a side window is even partially down on takeoff it causes the tail section to buffet.

New you are ready to check your engines:

It is far better to know what condition the engines are in before takeoff than to wait until you are off the ground. Remember, you're the fellow who is going to fly this airplane. Be confident that it is operating properly.

Check the direction of the nosewheel by looking at the polished area on the inside of the engine nacelles. See that it is straight before you run up the engines.

When you are ready for the run-up check, apply the power smoothly.

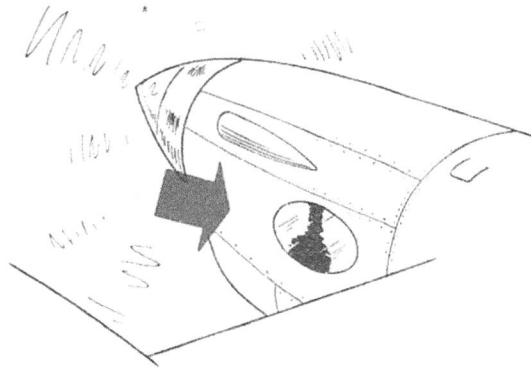

CHECK DIRECTION OF NOSEWHEEL IN POLISHED AREA ON NACELLES

RUN-UP CHECK

1. Pump the brakes so you can hold the airplane and then check the left engine.

2. Check the magnetos at 2300 rpm. If there is a drop of more than 100 rpm, return to the line.

Note: Check the magnetos with the propeller switches in AUTOMATIC and not in the selective FIXED PITCH. This eliminates the danger of forgetting to return the switches to AUTOMATIC. A takeoff with propellers in selective FIXED PITCH causes them to overspeed.

3. Propeller governors in full forward takeoff position.

4. At 2300 rpm, pull the left governor back until you get a reduction of 200 rpm.

5. Return the governor to the full-forward takeoff position, noting that it again attains 2300 rpm. If it does, the propeller is operating properly and ready for flight.

6. Check electrical system — voltmeter approximately 28 volts; ammeter charging below 50 amps.

Reduce the power on the left engine, maintaining at least 1200 rpm to keep the spark plugs from fouling. Check the right engine in the same manner, make a thorough cockpit check, and you are ready to go.

TAKEOFF

Roll the airplane a few feet down the runway so that the nosewheel will be in line when you apply power. Check its direction by means of the polished area on the inside of the engine nacelles.

No-flap takeoffs are preferred because you reach minimum single engine performance airspeed more rapidly this way than when you use flaps.

For maximum performance takeoffs, hold the airplane with brakes at the end of the runway until allowable takeoff manifold pressure and rpm have been reached. Then release the brakes. This way, the superchargers are in operation before you start your roll. Also, you have ample time to stop within the limits of the field in case of an emergency.

The tricycle landing gear gives the airplane a level flight attitude on the ground. During your roll down the runway, the wings offer a negative angle of attack and there is no tendency for the airplane to take off by itself. You will notice that there is no feeling of lightness as you reach takeoff speed. The airplane literally has to be lifted off the ground. At 80 mph ease the wheel back steadily and firmly. At 100 mph the airplane becomes airborne.

When you are certain you are airborne, retract the landing gear. The landing gear offers considerable drag when it is down. With the gear up, you quickly reach the minimum single engine airspeed of 120 mph.

Keep your hand on the throttles so that you can meet any emergency instantly.

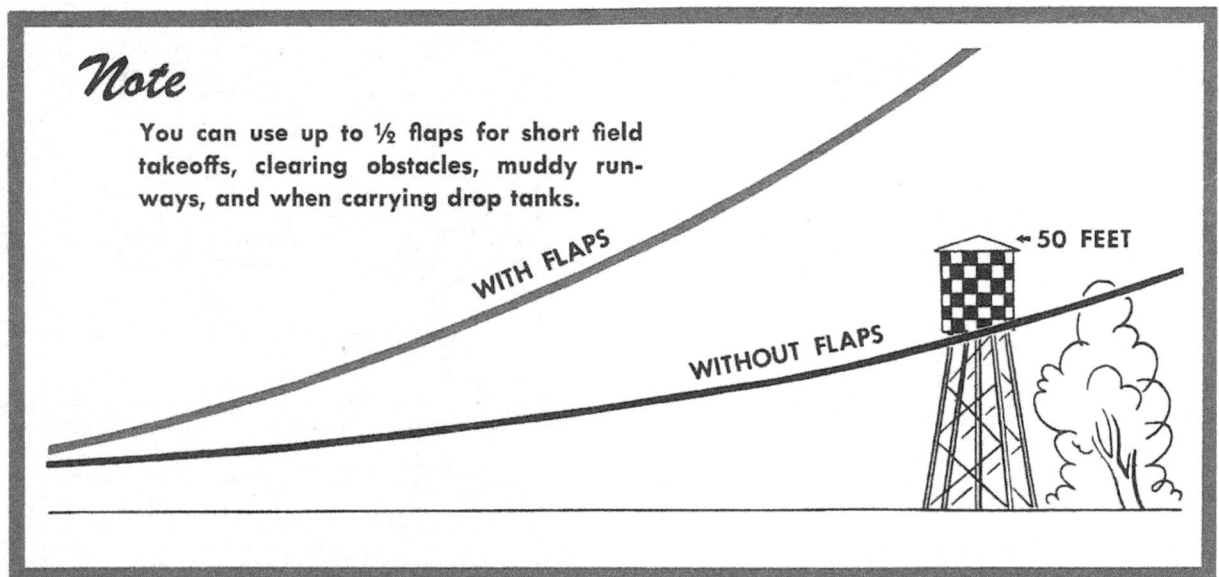

Note

You can use up to ½ flaps for short field takeoffs, clearing obstacles, muddy runways, and when carrying drop tanks.

WITH FLAPS

WITHOUT FLAPS

← 50 FEET

TAKEOFF PROCEDURE.

1. Pump brakes and hold.
2. Open the throttles to prescribed takeoff manifold pressure and rpm.
3. Release brakes.
4. When you are certain you are airborne retract the landing gear.

Tip: After takeoff from a muddy field, brake the wheels before retracting the landing gear. This prevents mud from being thrown into the wheelwells.

5. Reduce the power to prescribed climbing manifold pressure and rpm after you've reached sufficient airspeed and have cleared all obstacles.

Note: If you used flaps, retract them after you have at least 500 feet altitude.

6. Check your temperature readings and make any necessary adjustments.

OPERATING DATA

GRADE 100 FUEL

P-38 H, P-38 J and P-38 L:
V-1710-89 and V-1710-91 engines.
V-1710-111 and V-1710-113 engines.

	MANIFOLD PRESSURE	RPM
TAKEOFF	54"	3000
CLIMB	40"	2600
NORMAL CRUISE	30"	2300

P-38 F and P-38 G:
V-1710-49 and V-1710-53 engines.
V-1710-51 and V-1710-55 engines.

	MANIFOLD PRESSURE	RPM
TAKEOFF	45"	3000
CLIMB	35"	2600
NORMAL CRUISE	28"	2300

Due to the fluctuating demands of combat requirements, Grade 100 fuel is not always available for P-38 training.

The P-38 operates well on Grade 91 fuel provided you are familiar with and do not exceed its limitations.

Read these Technical Orders:

T.O. No. 02-1-38
T.O. No. 02-5A-66A

The operating chart on the right is recommended where normal operating conditions prevail. These figures apply to all P-38 series using Grade 91 fuel.

GRADE 91 FUEL

	MANIFOLD PRESSURE	RPM
TAKEOFF	45"	3000
CLIMB	35"	2600
NORMAL CRUISE	28"	2300

CLIMB

After takeoff, establish desired climbing manifold and rpm settings.

Make frequent checks on the temperatures and pressures and make the necessary adjustments.

Your most efficient climbing speed is between 155 mph and 175 mph. Try to keep the airspeed at 165 mph IAS.

You need little or no trim for rudder and aileron, but save your strength and relieve that nose heaviness with the elevator trim tab.

After you have established a normal climb, turn the electric fuel booster pumps OFF.

Important: If you are going to altitude, you must turn the electric booster pumps on again at approximately 12,000 feet.

CRUISE

Watch your gasoline supply carefully. Fly for the first 15 minutes on RES (reserve). Time each tank. Don't depend entirely upon the fuel quantity gages.

You will find the airplane trims easily and flies hands off.

Make it a habit frequently to check all the engine instruments for proper reading. After a while, you will be able to read all the instruments at a brief glance.

Learn to keep your head out of the cockpit

STALLS

In either power-on or power-off stalls with flaps and landing gear up, the airplane mushes straight ahead in a well controlled stall. With flaps and gear down, there is a slight tendency for one wing to drop. Under these conditions, the nose drops slightly and, as the airspeed increases, the wing comes up. There is no tendency to spin or whip off on one wing.

There is a noticeable vibration as you approach the stalling speed. The center section stalls first while the ailerons remain unstalled and effective. With power on there is excellent rudder control.

Practice stalls so that you know the feel of the controls near the stall and the indicated stalling speed of your airplane.

With power off, the P-38 stalls at approximately the following indicated airspeeds at the gross weights noted:

Flaps and gear up

15,000 lbs.	17,000 lbs.	19,000 lbs.
94 mph	100 mph	105 mph

Flaps and gear down

15,000 lbs.	17,000 lbs.	19,000 lbs.
69 mph	74 mph	78 mph

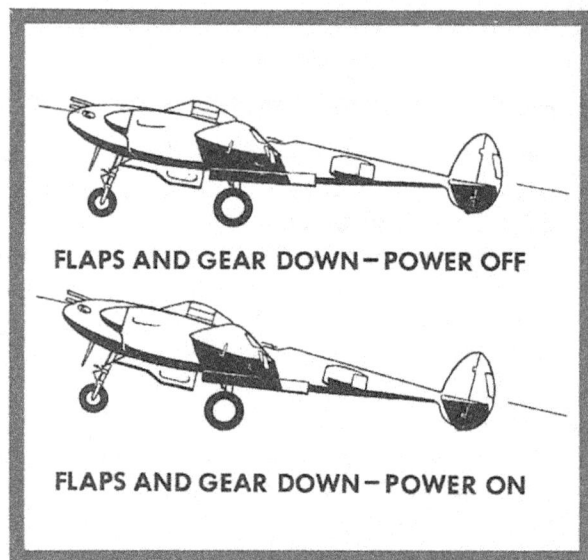

FLAPS AND GEAR DOWN—POWER OFF

FLAPS AND GEAR DOWN—POWER ON

Flight Restrictions

1. Snap rolls and spins.
2. Continuous inverted flight.
3. Don't exceed the airspeed or accelerations given on the DIVE LIMITS placard posted in the cockpit.
4. Don't exceed 3.5 negative G's. Excessive negative G's, as in inverted flight, cause the oil to leave the bottom of the crankcase and it does not furnish sufficient lubrication for the bearings.

5. Take extreme care during acrobatic maneuvers which require downward recovery (split-S). Twelve thousand feet in a P-38 isn't high.

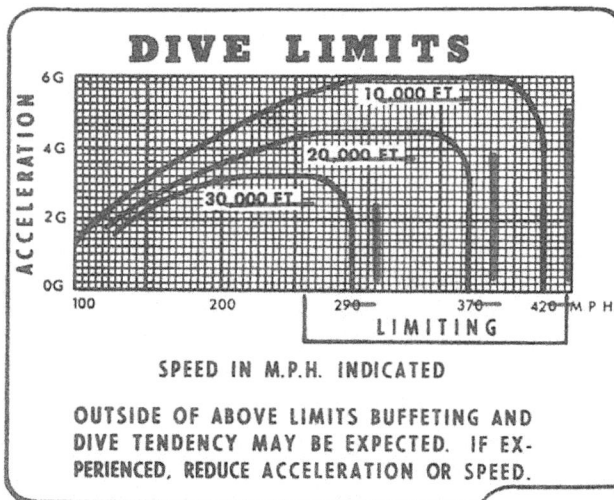

In early P-38 series, this placard is on the left side of the cockpit between the electric drop tank release box and the engine control stand. In later airplanes it is on the horizontal arm of the control column. It is there for your reference.

DIVE LIMITS

OUTSIDE OF ABOVE LIMITS BUFFETING AND DIVE TENDENCY MAY BE EXPECTED. IF EXPERIENCED, REDUCE ACCELERATION OR SPEED.

This has been designed to replace the above placard. The IAS red line at 20,000 feet has been changed and TAS is included to give you an estimate of your actual ground speed. The reason for these changes are shown in the chart on page 71.

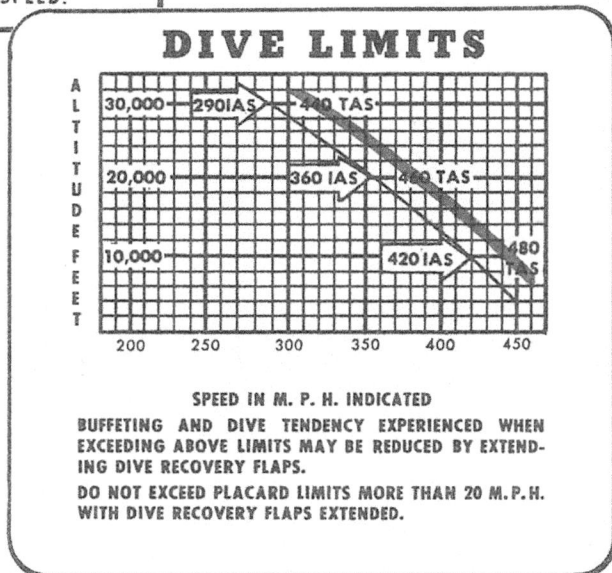

DIVE LIMITS

SPEED IN M. P. H. INDICATED
BUFFETING AND DIVE TENDENCY EXPERIENCED WHEN EXCEEDING ABOVE LIMITS MAY BE REDUCED BY EXTENDING DIVE RECOVERY FLAPS.
DO NOT EXCEED PLACARD LIMITS MORE THAN 20 M.P.H. WITH DIVE RECOVERY FLAPS EXTENDED.

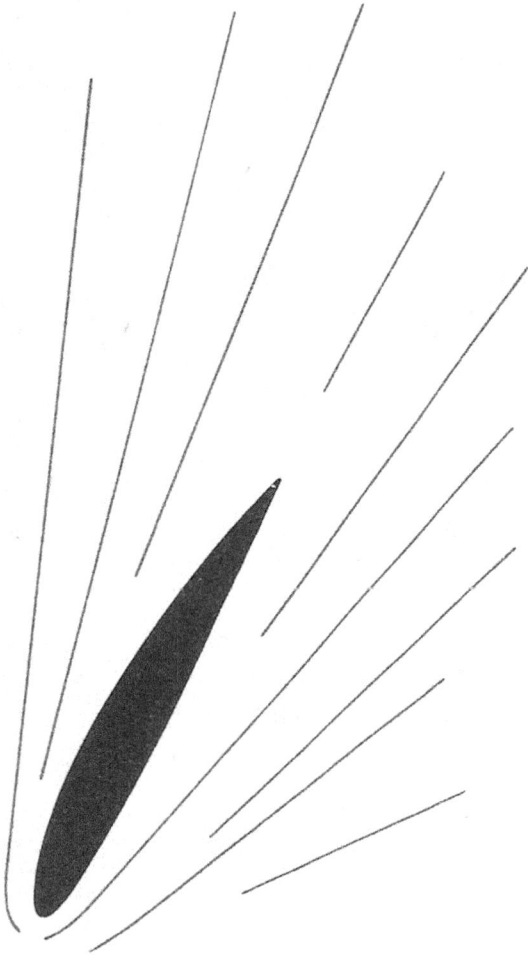

DIVES

In all high speed aircraft, particularly the P-38, you encounter a serious acceleration problem.

Previously you have flown airplanes that had a comparatively low terminal velocity and did not accelerate above a certain speed.

This is our problem: In high speed dives, the lack of resistance, due to the clean lines of the airplane, causes a tremendous acceleration if gravity is allowed to exert its full influence. As you approach the critical airspeed, the airplane becomes noseheavy and starts to buffet as if you were about to stall. Therefore, it is very foolhardy to point the P-38 straight down for any length of time. Adding to this problem of

acceleration is the problem of time required and space necessary to pull out of the dive and regain straight and level flight.

In your flying experience you have become aware of the futility of trying to recover from a stall by holding the stick back. The same situation exists here. In a high speed dive, only a few G's cause the airplane to buffet.

When it is necessary to point down, cut the power and enter the dive at a low airspeed.

Normal Dive Recovery

If you have allowed yourself to build up excessive airspeed in a dive, follow this recommended procedure for recovery:

1. Pull back the throttles (If you haven't already done so).

2. Apply sufficient back pressure until you feel a slight nibble in the wheel. Any further pressure causes the airplane to buffet and defeats your purpose of trying to pull out.

3. Use only a few degrees of elevator trim tab to help you.

Caution

USE THE ELEVATOR TAB WITH EXTREME CARE. TOO MUCH TRIM CAUSES A TAIL-HEAVY CONDITION.

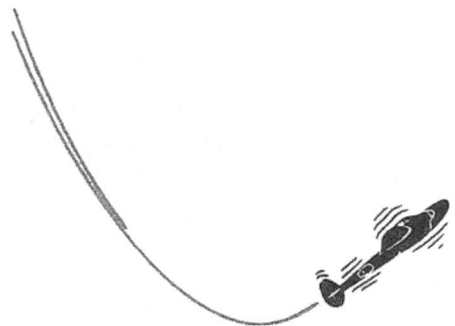

Relationship of Airspeed and Altitude

The maximum safe airspeeds for the P-38 at different altitudes are given in the accompanying chart. Notice in the chart that the airspeeds are given in terms of IAS (indicated airspeed) and TAS (true airspeed). Notice also how greatly these two figures differ. At 30,000 feet, for example, 300 mph IAS means you are actually traveling 480 mph TAS. A good thumbnail rule to remember in making this airspeed correction is:

Increase IAS 2% per 1000 feet. This is the way it works out in the above example: 2% for each 1000 feet in 30,000 feet is 60%; 60% of 300 IAS is 180 mph; add 300 and 180 mph and you have 480 mph TAS.

The red line on the airspeed indicator of the P-38 is placed at 420 mph. That does not mean 420 mph IAS at any altitude. That is simply the speed at which the load on the wings and other structural parts reaches the maximum they are designed to carry.

Notice in the chart that above 10,000 feet the indicated red line is less than 420 mph IAS and continues to decrease with an increase of altitude. At 30,000 feet, your safe maximum IAS is 290 mph.

In other words, the red line is not a fixed figure, but a **variable** figure—variable with altitude. The higher you go, the lower the maximum allowable IAS.

Many pilots fail to realize this great difference between IAS and TAS at high altitudes. Don't be fooled. Study these figures carefully. **Never exceed these airspeeds.**

In the case of high speed fighter planes, a new factor enters the picture which makes diving unsafe at high altitudes long before the usual red line is reached. This new factor is compressibility. It is the reason for the variable red-line speed as given in the chart.

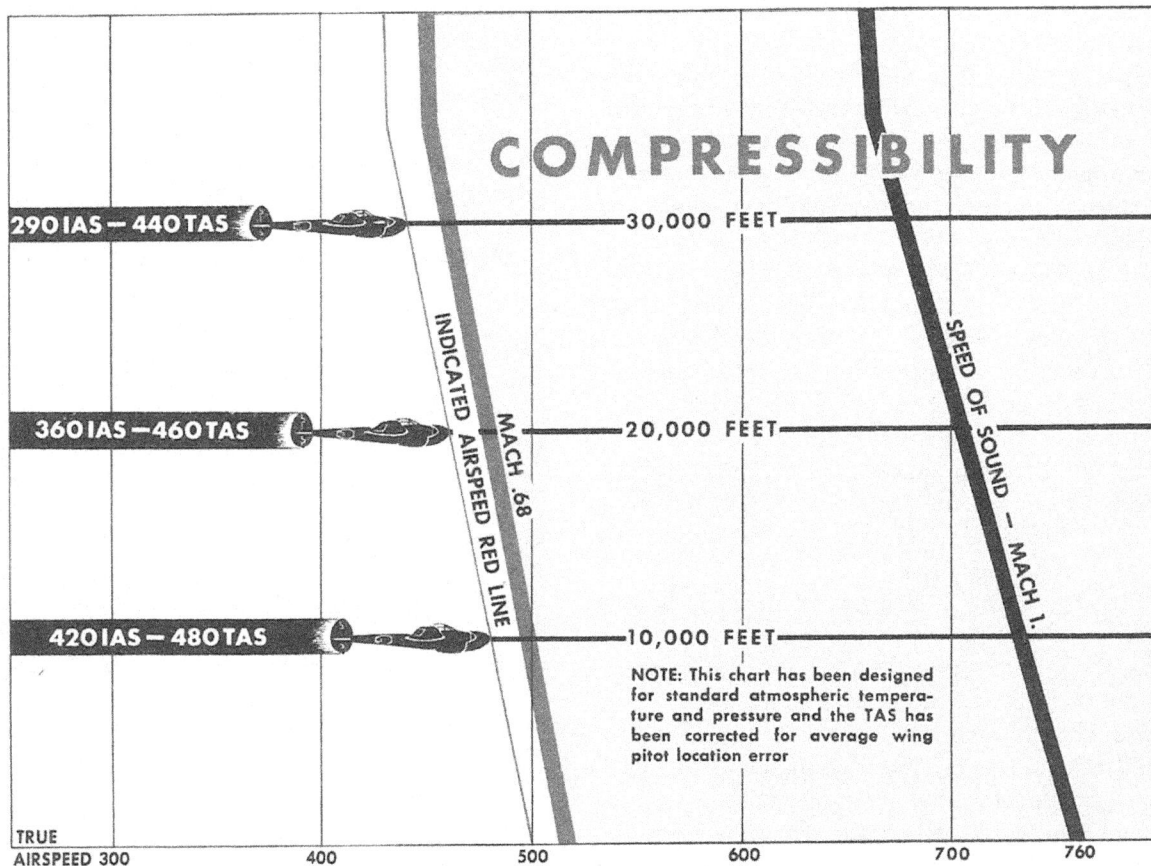

COMPRESSIBILITY

290 IAS — 440 TAS ———— 30,000 FEET

360 IAS — 460 TAS ———— 20,000 FEET

420 IAS — 480 TAS ——— 10,000 FEET

INDICATED AIRSPEED RED LINE

MACH .68

SPEED OF SOUND — MACH 1.

NOTE: This chart has been designed for standard atmospheric temperature and pressure and the TAS has been corrected for average wing pitot location error

TRUE
AIRSPEED 300   400   500   600   700   760

COMPRESSIBILITY

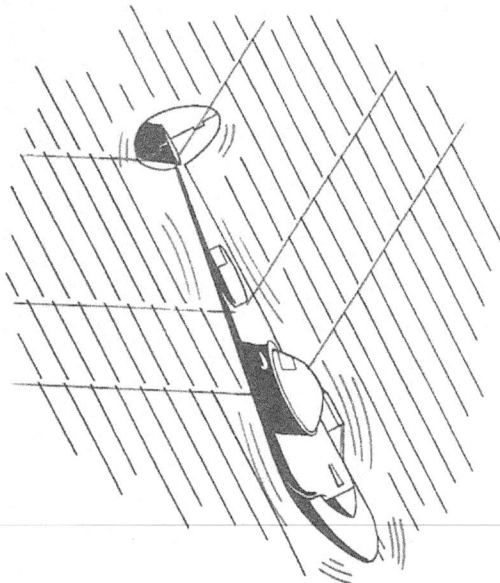

Since extremely high airplane speeds have been developed only in recent years, the phenomenon of compressibility is still pretty much of a mystery. Scientists and engineers know comparatively little about it and dive tests are still being run to prove or disprove the many theories about it. Here we attempt to give you a pilot's explanation about compressibility in a P-38; one that will help you understand this phenomenon and impress upon you the importance of avoiding it.

About all that is known for certain is this. When an airplane approaches the speed of sound, it loses its efficiency. Compression waves or shock waves develop on the wings and other surfaces of the airplane.

Although there is a great deal of disagreement as to **what** happens when compressibility is reached, and **why**, there is no question as to the **result**, so far as the pilot is concerned.

The lift characteristics of the airplane are greatly reduced and the stability, control, and trim are affected.

Each type high speed fighter plane has its own individual compressibility characteristics. In your P-38, the first effect as you approach compressibility is that the airplane becomes

noseheavy. The control wheel moves forward and becomes increasingly difficult to pull back. At this stage, an uncontrollable buffeting and vibrating develops. If the speed of the airplane isn't checked and control regained, it is possible that the terrific vibrations of the shock waves may cause structural failure, or the airplane may crash while still in the compressibility dive.

Relationship of Compressibility to the Speed of Sound

Under standard temperature and atmospheric conditions, the speed of sound at sea level is 760 mph. An airplane goes into compressibility before actually reaching the speed of sound. This speed varies in different airplanes depending upon the individual design of the airplane.

The speed at which an airplane enters compressibility, in ratio to the speed of sound, is technically known as its **Mach number** (pronounced Mock and named after the man who did considerable research in this field).

One of the most important things to remember about compressibility is that the speed of sound varies with altitude. Note these approximate figures:

At sea level, sound travels 760 mph.
At 30,000 feet, sound travels 670 mph.

35,000 feet → 670 mph

Sea Level ————→ 760 mph

THE SPEED OF SOUND DECREASES WITH AN INCREASE OF ALTITUDE

Therefore, the higher you go, the sooner you reach the speed of sound, and the lower your safe IAS will be.

In a high speed dive from altitude, you get into compressibility before you reach the 420 mph IAS red line on the airspeed indicator.

COMPRESSIBILITY DIVE

It is possible to come out of compressibility if you don't go too far. This all depends on the circumstances of the dive; the angle, starting altitude, airspeed, and the point at which compressibility was reached.

Then there is this to consider; while in compressibility you have no control over the airplane. Also it is possible to aggravate your situation and make it a lot worse. All that you can do is pull back the throttles (if they aren't already back), hold the stick as steady as possible with some back pressure, and then ride it through until you decelerate enough, at a lower altitude, to reduce your speed below the red line speed given in the chart. This usually means an uncontrolled dive of between 10,000

feet and 15,000 feet, depending upon circumstances.

The exact altitude you drop and the length of time you are in compressibility depends to a great extent upon the angle of dive in which you encountered compressibility.

Only after you have lost enough speed and altitude will you come out of compressibility and regain control of your airplane. At that point, with the airplane again under control, you can **begin** to come out of your dive.

Note that last sentence carefully. You can then **begin** to come out of your dive—that's after losing 10,000 feet to 15,000 feet. If at that point you still have sufficient altitude for a controlled dive recovery, you're okay. If you don't . . . ?

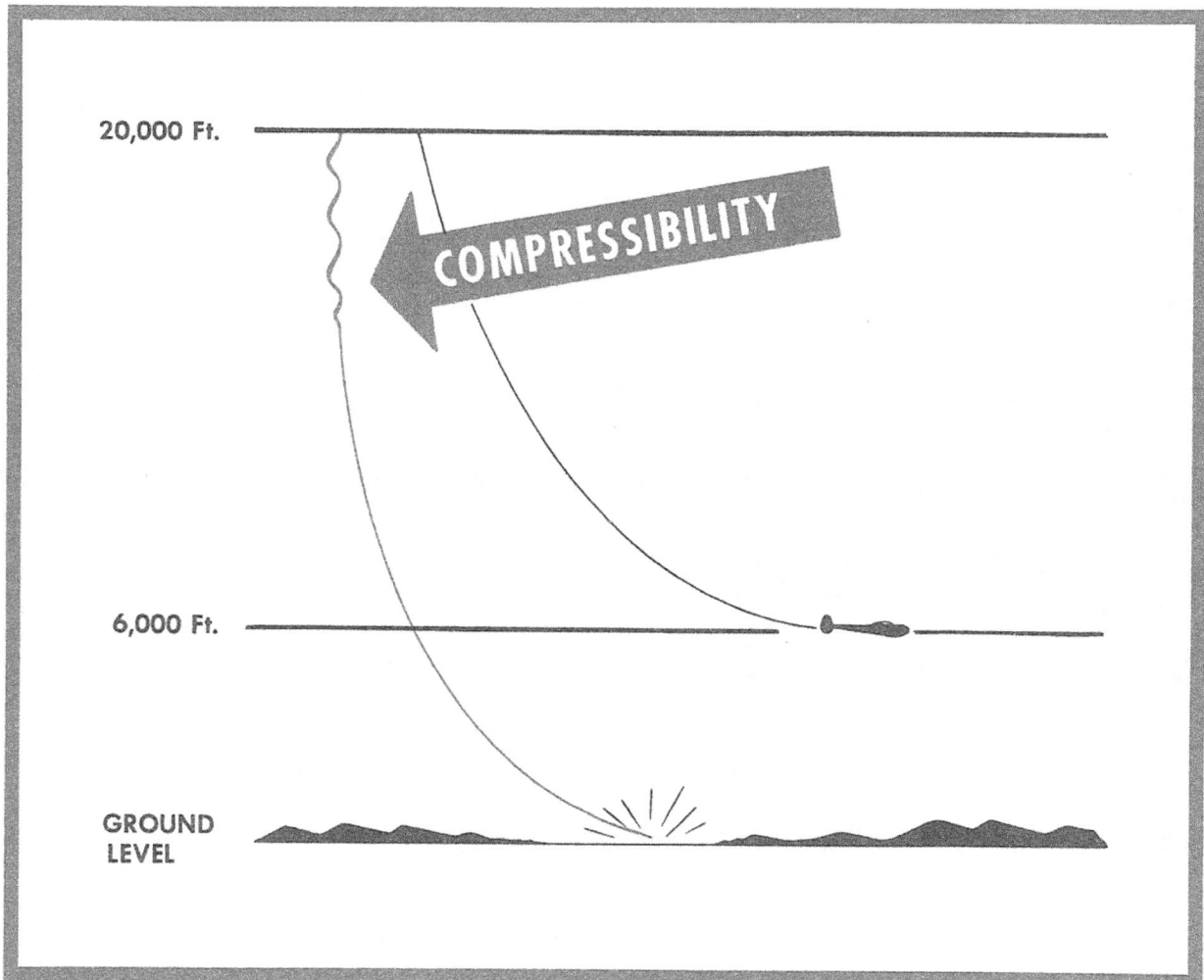

COMPRESSIBILITY RECOVERY PROCEDURE

Most important of all, **don't get into compressibility.** But if you do get into compressibility in a high-speed dive, don't get excited. Keep cool; and follow this recommended recovery procedure:

1. Cut the power **immediately.** To get out of compressibility you have to lose airspeed, so pull your throttles back.

2. Hold the stick as steady as you can, maintaining a slight amount of back pressure. Too much back pressure will greatly increase the tail buffeting.

3. Use only a few degrees of elevator trim tab. Too much trim causes the airplane to pull out abruptly when a lower airspeed and altitude is reached.

4. As the airplane slowly but steadily decelerates with power off, and you get into the lower altitudes where the speed of sound is greater, the buffeting decreases and you can regain control of the airplane.

5. Pull out of the dive in a normal recovery. **Don't pull out abruptly.** Take it as easy as altitude permits.

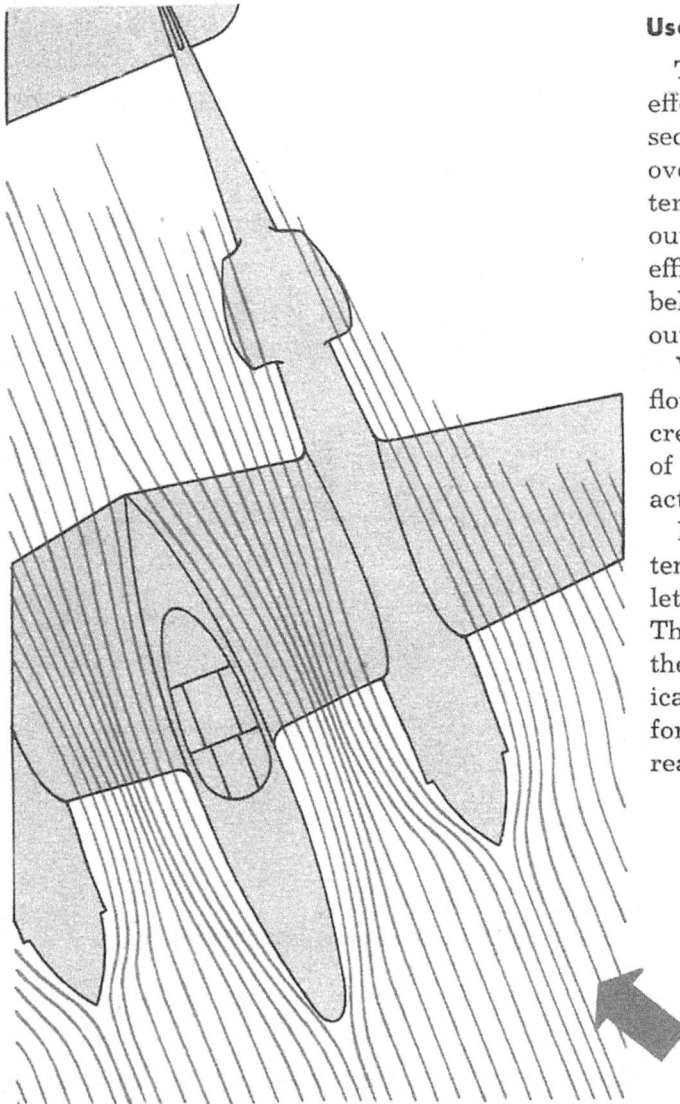

Use of Dive Flaps

The gondola and nacelle create a venturi effect so that the air passing over the center section of the wing travels much faster than over the outboard section. Therefore, the center section goes into compressibility while the outboard section still has some aerodynamic efficiency. That is why the dive flaps are placed below and behind the leading-edge of the wing, outboard of the nacelles.

When you lower the dive flaps, they spoil the flow of air under the wing, creating an increase in lift efficiency on the upper surface of the wing. This destroys the noseheavy characteristics which are found in high speed dives.

It is recommended that the dive flaps be extended as soon as the dive is begun rather than let the speed build up and then extend the flaps. This provides much better control throughout the dive and minimizes the chances of mechanical failure. You don't have to lower them before you start the dive, but simply before you reach compressibility.

VENTURI EFFECT

CAUSED BY GONDOLA

AND NACELLES

SPINS

Deliberate spinning is prohibited. If the P-38 is allowed to spin, after 2 or 3 turns it tends to flatten out. When this occurs, the controls are forced back and you must use engine power to help get the wheel forward. Before flattening out, you can make a normal recovery without power. To make a normal recovery from a spin, apply full opposite rudder and ease the wheel forward.

Note

If you accidentally fall into an inverted spin, pull the stick back. This gets your nose down and develops a normal spin.

Recover from a normal spin in the following manner:

1. Pull back the throttles.
2. Full opposite rudder until spin stops.
3. Ease wheel forward.

DON'T USE AILERON AGAINST THE TURN. THIS HAS A BLANKETING ACTION ON THE RUDDERS.

SINGLE ENGINE PRACTICE

Sometime after your first 10 hours in P-38 you will practice single engine flight. This is done from cruising airspeed at not less than 8000 feet altitude. Your flight leader flies alongside and directs you by radio.

You will find that the P-38 flies very well on one engine. Using normal rated power, it can climb above 20,000 feet and have a TAS greater than 225 mph.

In practicing single engine flight, cut the right engine. The generator in most P-38's is on the left engine. With the left engine dead the generator is not operating and the battery will go dead in about 30 minutes. If your airplane has two generators that are on and working you can practice feathering either propeller.

Check the ammeter and the voltmeter before you cut the engine.

Practice the procedure for single engine performance as though it were an actual engine failure. This prepares you for such an emergency.

The following practice procedure is designed to take care of an engine failure just after take-off or in flight.

Close throttle of right engine. This simulates an engine failure. Immediately do the following:

1. Reduce power to gain directional control. Correct yaw with rudder immediately, applying as much power as you can hold.

2. Check to be sure landing gear is in UP position.

3. Release drop tanks (or bombs).

4. Trim rudder to take pressure off rudder pedal.

5. Move mixture control of bad engine to IDLE CUT-OFF. Be certain you pull the mixture control of the bad engine.

6. Feather propeller of bad engine.

7. Fuel booster pump OFF.

8. Close coolant and oil shutters of dead engine.

Note

In single engine practice, do not turn off fuel supply or ignition of dead engine.

Use as little power as necessary from the good engine. Don't burn it up. With 2600 rpm and 35″ manifold pressure, you can maintain an air-speed of 150 mph to 200 mph.

To Unfeather Propeller and Start Engine

Be sure feather switch is in NORMAL position. This is important. You cannot unfeather unless the feather switch is in NORMAL.

1. Throttle cracked and propeller governor control lever full rearward.

2. Move propeller switch to INCREASE RPM. The propeller will start windmilling. When the tachometer registers 600 to 800 rpm, return the propeller switch to AUTOMATIC.

3. Move mixture control to AUTO RICH. Engine will start.

4. Run the engine at 20″ Hg. and 1500 rpm. Resume normal operation when the coolant temperature reaches 85°C and the oil temperature is at least 50°C.

5. Trim tabs NEUTRAL.

6. Adjust oil and coolant shutters (switches in AUTOMATIC on P-38H through P-38L).

Check!

IF THE ENGINE DOESN'T START, CHECK THE FOLLOWING:

1. FEATHER SWITCH IN NORMAL
2. FUEL SELECTOR TO FULLEST TANK
3. IGNITION SWITCH ON

LANDING

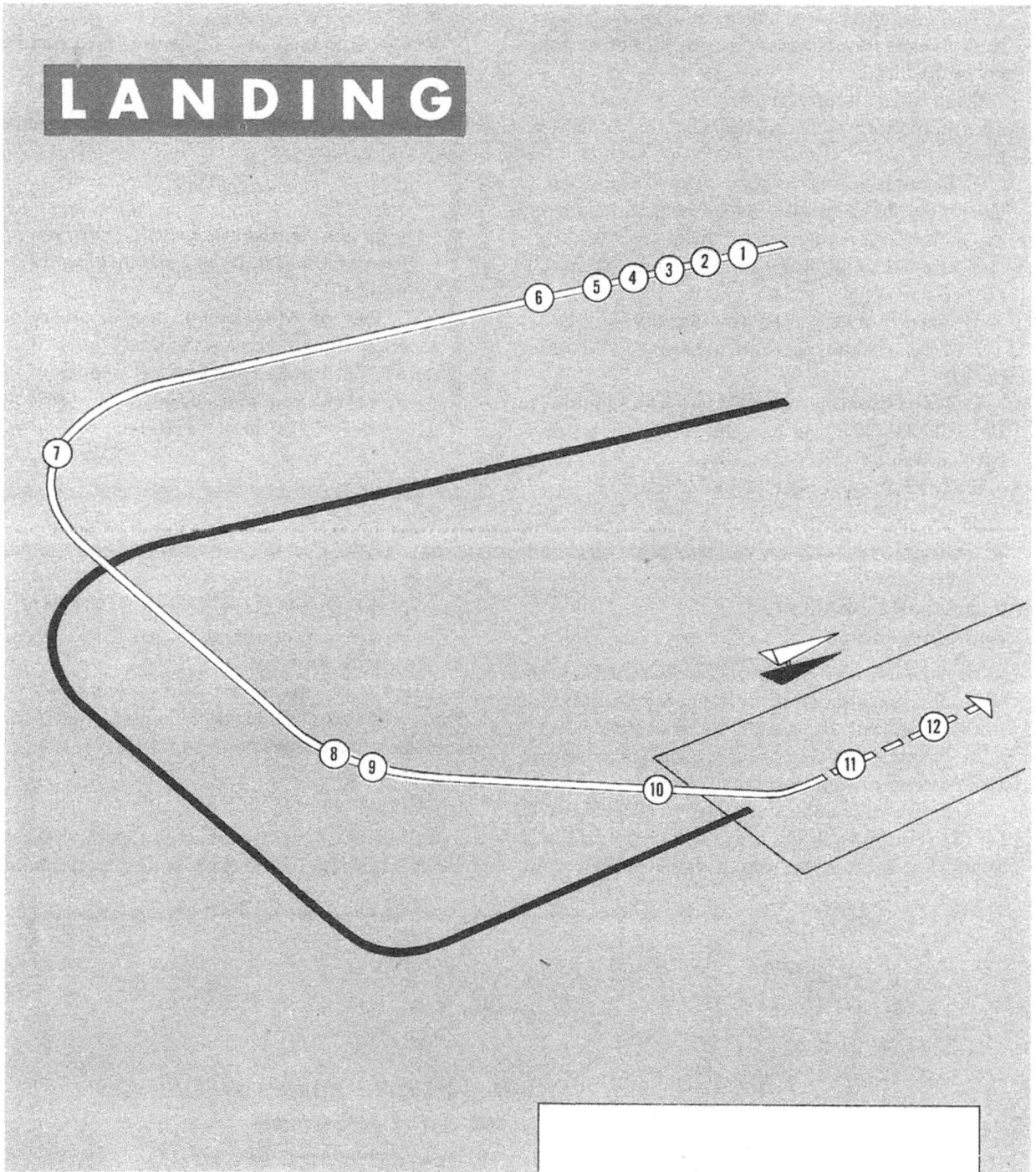

Don't be tricycle-gear conscious. The P-38
lands in the same attitude as the airplane with
conventional landing gear.

Land on the 2 main wheels. The nosewheel
settles of its own accord.

Landing Procedure

1. Fuel selectors to fullest tanks.
2. Fuel booster pumps ON.
3. Mixture in AUTO RICH.
4. Propellers at 2600 rpm.
5. Intercooler shutters OPEN (if installed). This is not necessary during cold weather operation.
6. Slow up on downwind leg to 175 mph and lower landing gear. Don't cut the throttles to slow down. Reduce them gradually and maintain at least 15″ manifold pressure. If you cut the throttles, the engine will backfire and possibly load up.

Make the following thorough check to be certain gear is down and locked:

Hydraulic pressure . . . . returned to normal.
Hand pump . . . . resists operation.
Position indicator . . . . wheels down.
Warning horn . . . silent when throttles back.
Warning light . . . . . out when throttles back.
Polished area . . . . nosewheel down.

7. Turn on base leg at 150 mph.
8. Make final turn into field at 150 mph.
9. Drop full flaps. Lift the trigger through the quadrant notch to place the flap handle in the full DOWN position.

Tip: When lowering the flaps, keep forward pressure on the stick, as the extension of the flaps causes you to gain altitude.

10. Establish glide at 130 mph, carrying at least 15″ manifold pressure. Gradually reduce power and airspeed to 110 mph for glide, coming over the fence at 100 mph.

Perfect your landing approach technique. It requires skill and judgement and is one of the tests that determine a good pilot.

Don't drag your approach in from miles back. On long, low approaches, an engine failure leaves you in an embarrassing situation.

Too high an approach is just as bad. Don't look as if you are going to dive bomb the field.

Tip: On the final leg, pump the toe brakes to build up hydraulic pressure so that you will be sure to have brakes when you need them. This also insures that your brakes are not locked when landing. Land with your heels on the floor. Keep your feet off the brakes. Roll back elevator trim tab to relieve pressure on the stick.

11. Make contact between 90 mph and 100 mph.

Land on the 2 main wheels, holding the nosewheel off the ground. With full flaps down you can't drag the rudder fins on the runway. With ½ flaps or less you can.

12. After contacting the runway, keep the airplane straight. Steer with the rudders as long as they are effective. Do not use brakes unless necessary. Then apply them on and off.

Tip: Be prepared to encounter prop wash when landing behind another airplane. If you hit prop wash, correct immediately! Don't sit there fat, dumb, and happy while the airplane does a snap roll.

Make every approach and landing with the same care and concern as you did on your first solo.

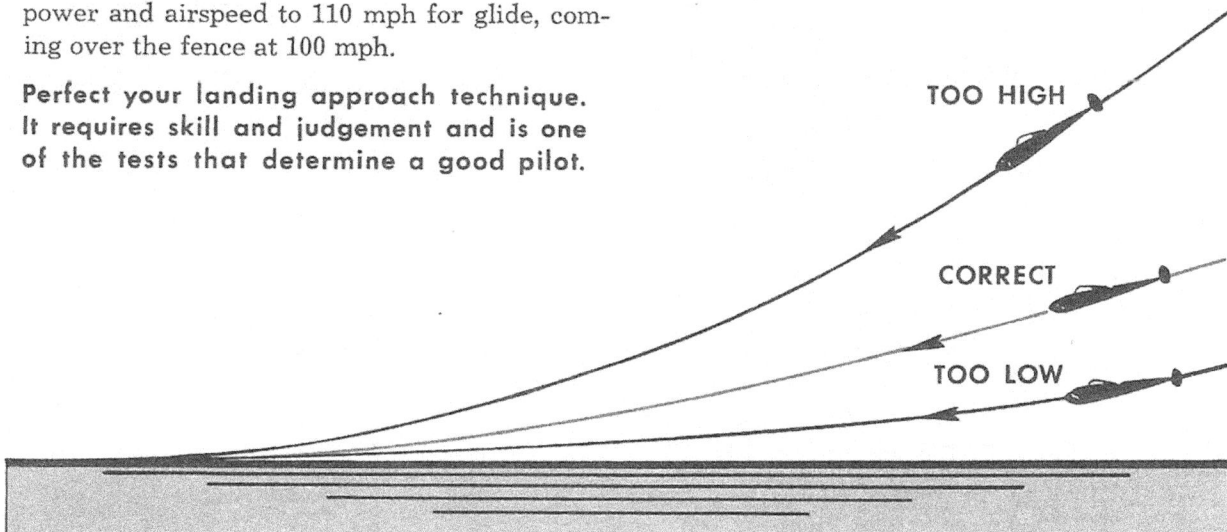

TOO HIGH

CORRECT

TOO LOW

GO-AROUND PROCEDURE

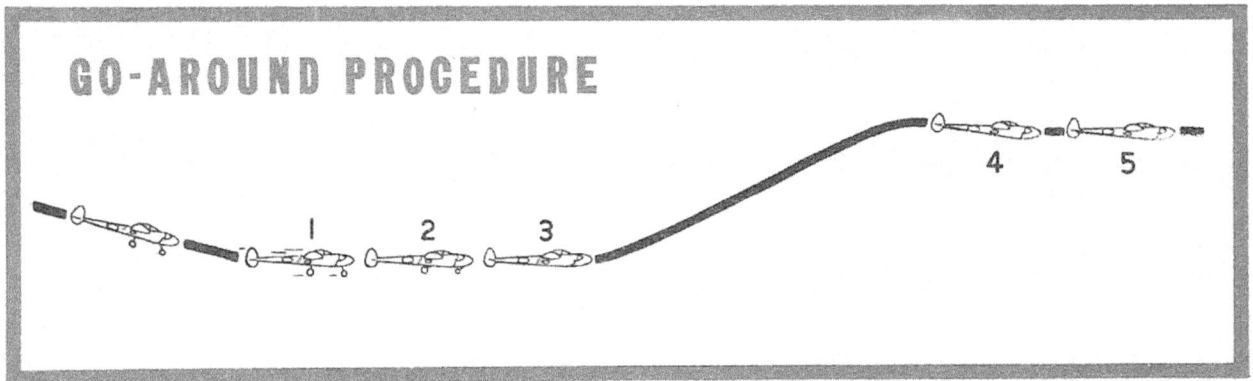

If you overshoot and cannot land in the first third of the field, go around.

If for any reason you do not feel that everything is just right, go around.

You will not be criticized. It will be considered good judgment. But try to make up your mind early. Don't wait until you are half-way down the runway.

In going around, use the following procedure:

1. Set throttle to takeoff manifold pressure. **Important:** Maximum rpm 3000.
2. Retract the landing gear.
3. Climb straight ahead and gain at least 500 feet altitude.
4. Lower nose slightly and build up airspeed.
5. Milk up the flaps.

Don't try to fly around the field with gear and flaps down; don't turn until flaps are up.

CROSSWIND LANDINGS

A crosswind landing in a P-38 presents no problem because of the tricycle landing gear.

With the tricycle landing gear the center of gravity is **forward** of the main wheels. Once the wheels have touched the ground, the P-38 rolls straight down the runway. It will not groundloop.

On the final approach, crab or lower a wing into the wind, or use a combination of both.

Be sure you straighten out before making contact. Do not land in a crabbed or one-wing-low attitude. The gear was not built to take excessive side stress.

Immediately upon landing, put the nose-wheel on the runway to obtain directional stability and roll straight down the runway.

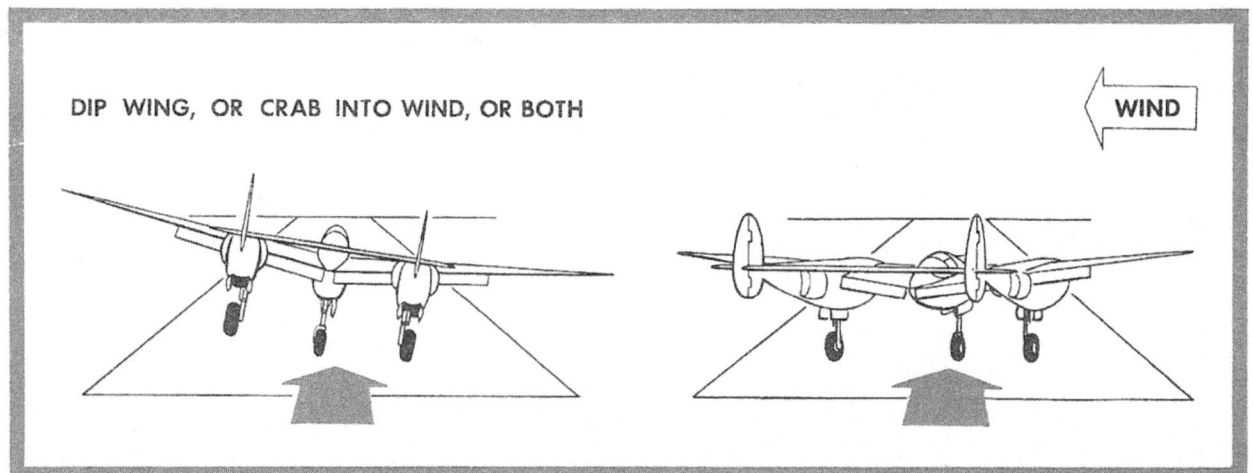

DIP WING, OR CRAB INTO WIND, OR BOTH — WIND

AFTER LANDING

Keep the airplane straight with rudder. Avoid unnecessary usage of the brakes.

Don't raise the flaps until you have reached the end of the runway. This helps you slow the airplane.

After you have slowed down, pull your flaps up, turn the booster pumps OFF; push the propeller governors full forward, and set the trim tabs to 0. Then place the oil and coolant shutters in FULL OPEN. This helps keep the temperatures down while you taxi.

Don't set the parking brakes after you have returned to the line. The brake discs get hot while taxiing and will freeze if you set them. After you have turned the engines off, hold the brakes until chocks have been placed.

To Stop the Engines

1. Open throttles to 1500 rpm.

Note: Hold this for a few seconds to burn out any impurities that may have collected on the spark plugs while taxiing.

2. Move mixture controls to IDLE CUT-OFF.

3. When the propellers stop rotating, turn all switches OFF.

NIGHT TRANSITION

You will do almost all your flying during daylight hours. But there will be times when you take off in the wee hours of the morning and sometimes in the late afternoon, coming home after dark.

Night flying in a P-38 presents no problem. But there are several precautions you must remember. Here are a few tips to help you:

Before takeoff

Equip yourself with a flashlight.

Make the **Special Check for Night Flying.**
Check to see that aileron boost is OFF (if installed).
Set the altimeter to ZERO.
Use oxygen to improve your night vision.
Establish radio contact.
Taxi slowly, alternating the use of wing lights.
Turn the wing lights off if a plane is landing.
Get radio permission to take off.
Pick a point at the end of the runway to keep you straight on your takeoff run.

82

During flight

Proceed to your assigned zone and altitude.

Remain in your zone until called by the tower.

Keep your head on a swivel.

Frequently check your instruments and fuel supply. It is recommended that aileron boost remain OFF during all night flying.

A turn can change contact flying to instrument flying. If you lose the horizon, immediately go on instruments until you definitely establish your attitude. Don't fly by the seat of your pants.

Always keep the field in sight.

Don't make steep turns at any time.

Important: If radio contact fails, turn on your landing light and point your plane at the tower. When they give you a green light, go in and land.

If an emergency occurs, immediately start your letdown for landing and turn on your landing lights. This is your emergency clearance.

Don't be alarmed by the glow of the turbo-superchargers.

Landing

When you retard the throttles, sparks and perhaps flames will appear. Don't be alarmed. It's there in the daytime, too, but you can't see it.

Maintain 1500 feet in the pattern until you turn into the final approach.

Use of landing lights and floodlights is optional. If there is haze or dust over the field, a blackout landing is recommended.

Go-around procedure is the same.

A safety officer will be in the tower or in a radio truck. Help yourself by observing his instructions.

INSTRUMENT FLYING

Under the present system, you receive instrument training under a hood while flying formation with your instructor. The instructor has contact with you by radio and can tell you to come out from under the hood if there are any airplanes in the vicinity. As a precaution in case of radio failure, come out from under the hood every 3 minutes and look around.

SECTION 4 EMERGENCY

ENGINE FAILURE

When an engine conks out on a single engine fighter, the first thing the pilot does is look around for a place to make a forced landing. If he happens to be above an overcast, rough terrain, or a heavy sea, his best bet is to hit the silk. If his engine fails on takeoff he has no other choice but to glide straight ahead. You, as a P-38 pilot, are not faced with this problem. If an engine fails after takeoff or during flight, you still have a good single engine airplane under you.

The same procedure as outlined in **Single Engine Practice** is the procedure to use in case an engine fails during flight or after takeoff. **(Refer to Single Engine Practice Procedure.)**

The minimum single engine airspeed at which you can fly the P-38 is 120 mph with the landing gear up. It can happen that one engine quits on takeoff when you don't have 120 mph with the gear up. Here are the rules to remember:

If an engine fails, or there is an irregularity, between the start of the takeoff run and 120 mph IAS, cut both throttles and stop.

If you cannot stop on the runway, retract the gear and slide in. Use the landing gear emergency release knob to lift the control handle.

If an engine fails after you have left the ground and the landing gear is up, and you

have a minimum of 120 mph IAS, use the same procedure you learned in **Single Engine Practice.** The most important thing to remember is the first step. Come back on the power, gain directional control with rudder, and then apply as much power as you can hold. Use rudder and not aileron to correct the initial yaw. Use of aileron increases the drag on the dead engine side. Don't apply so much power on the live engine that you can't hold the airplane.

The landing gear, when down, offers 60% of the total drag. Be sure the landing gear has been retracted, or is on its way up. An IAS greater than 120 mph is what you are striving for. Put the nose down to gain extra speed.

Sacrifice Altitude for Airspeed

Try to maintain a level climb away from the field. Don't get excited and try to turn back and land. Get plenty of altitude and fly around until the ship feels comfortable. You may be able to find out the trouble and restart the engine. If not, with the assistance of an experienced pilot in the tower you can take your time and make a well planned single engine landing.

NEVER TURN INTO A DEAD ENGINE AT LOW ALTITUDE OR LOW AIRSPEED.

RESTRICTED

Single Engine Range

For maximum single engine range, fly as low as safety permits. Use the lowest power which maintains an IAS of approximately 160 mph.

Use fuel from the dead engine side first. This lessens the load and reduces the trim.

Caution: Your range and time in flight on one engine is less than the range and time in flight on two engines.

With drop tanks installed, use the fuel from the tank nearest the dead engine. Drop them when empty if it is necessary to increase your range.

If the left engine has failed, and you do not have a generator on the right engine, take action as indicated under Electrical Failure.

Single Engine Landing

If you have to make a single engine landing and are carrying drop tanks, release them over an unpopulated area. If your airplane has aileron boost control, make sure it has been turned OFF so that you have all available hydraulic pressure to lower landing gear and flaps.

You can maintain altitude on single engine with landing gear down.

However, do not attempt to fly the P-38 with full flaps and gear down on one engine. It will not maintain altitude.

The single engine approach differs from the normal approach in the following respects:

1. Use a minimum of 140 mph IAS: 150 mph desired.

2. Always turn into the live engine.

3. Enter traffic pattern keeping your altitude above 1500 feet.

You will make a slightly larger traffic pattern than is normal due to the slower rate of turn on single engine.

4. Lower your landing gear on the base leg.

The extension time will be doubled (or approximately 30 seconds) because only one hydraulic pump is working.

5. Pull the flap trigger through the notch and lower half flaps on the final approach. Estimate ½ flaps if no position indicator is installed.

Keep your airspeed above 120 mph on the final approach until you are ready to flare out.

6. Roll rudder trim tab to 0.

Prevent yaw with rudder and minimum use of aileron.

7. When you are certain you can make the field with power off, then lower full flaps and come over the end of the runway at 110 mph.

8. Make a normal landing.

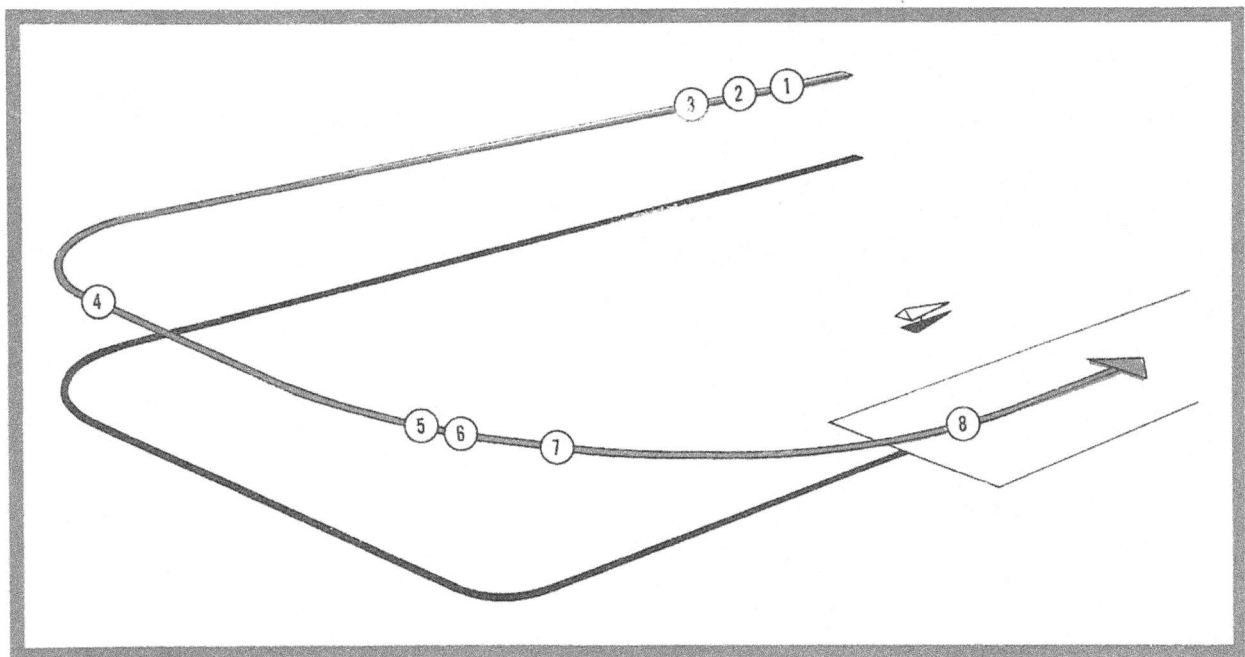

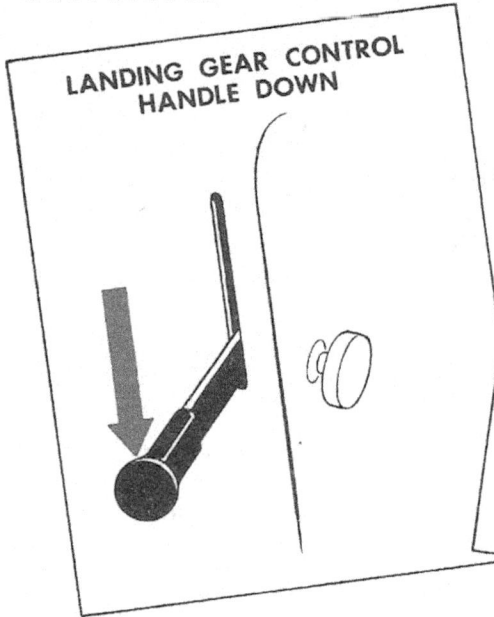

LANDING GEAR CONTROL HANDLE DOWN

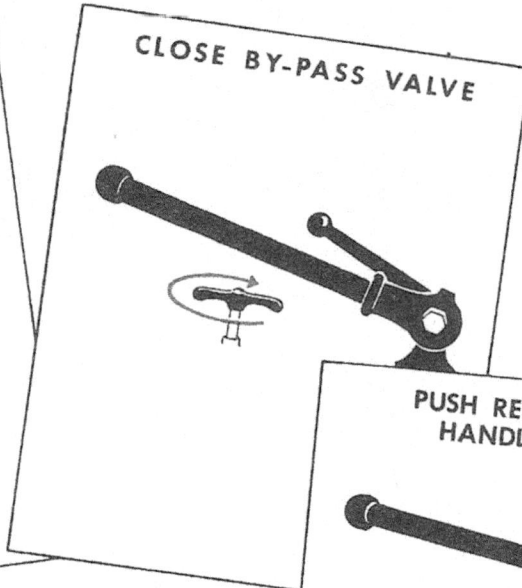

CLOSE BY-PASS VALVE

TO
LOWER
LANDING GEAR

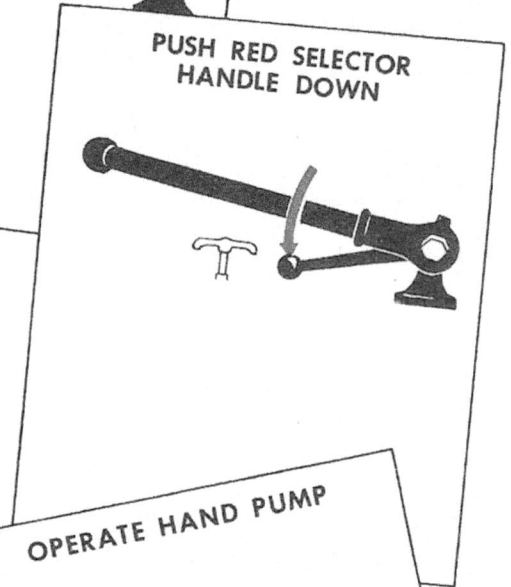

PUSH RED SELECTOR HANDLE DOWN

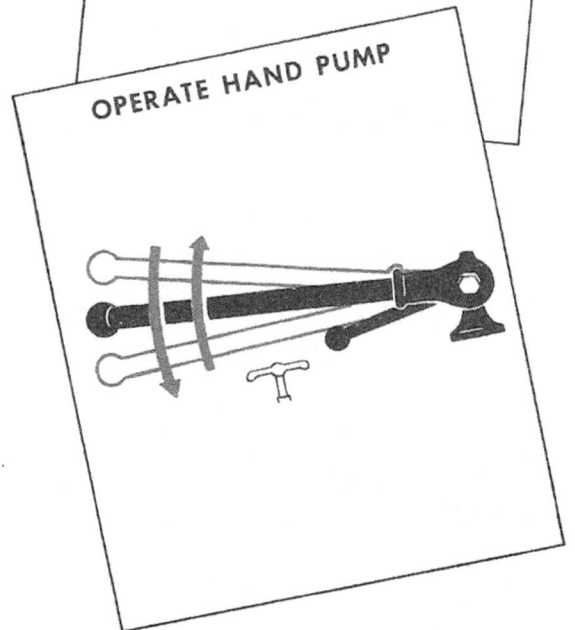

OPERATE HAND PUMP

HYDRAULIC FAILURE

Auxiliary System

Two conditions are usually the cause of hydraulic system failure. Either the engine hydraulic pump has gone out or there is a break in the hydraulic line. If the engine pump goes out there is still hydraulic fluid in the system and you can extend the gear and the flaps with the auxiliary hand pump. It is necessary, however, that you turn OFF the coolant override switches and aileron boost control. No other action except pumping is required.

The engine pumps drain the hydraulic fluid from the top two-thirds of the hydraulic reservoir while the hand pump drains from the bottom third. So, if there is a leak in the hydraulic system, only the top two-thirds can drain out. This leaves you the bottom third; enough hydraulic fluid to lower gear and flaps, with the hand pump supplying the pressure.

This auxiliary system uses the same lines as the normal hydraulic system.

Emergency Extension System

If the main hydraulic reservoir is empty or the lines are broken, you cannot build up any pressure with the hand pump alone. Use the emergency extension system.

NOTE: Coolant overide switches and aileron boost valve must be off to operate auxiliary hand pump.

This system is completely independent of the normal system. It has separate hydraulic lines and its own hydraulic reservoir. The hand pump is its power supply. After you have opened the system, all you need to lower the gear and flaps is a little elbow grease.

Since this system works off a separate set of hydraulic lines, there is no indication of pressure on the hydraulic pressure gage.

There is sufficient hydraulic fluid in the emergency system for only one operation. You can lower the landing gear **and that is all.** You can't retract the gear with this system.

A by-pass valve and selector valve (red handle) are on the floor to the right of your seat. When you close the by-pass valve, you shut off the regular hydraulic lines and open the lines from the emergency reservoir. Place the red handle down and the emergency fluid flows into the lines. The P-38 J and P-38 L series do not have the by-pass valve. The red handle incorporates the action of the by-pass valve.

Use the following procedure to lower the landing gear:

1. Coolant override switches OFF (if installed).

2. Aileron boost control OFF (if installed).

3. Landing gear control handle DOWN.

4. Close the by-pass valve by turning it clockwise.

5. Place the red handle in the DOWN position.

6. Operate the hand pump.

Pumping may be difficult at first because the wheel doors have to be forced open.

Tip: With the landing gear control hand in the DOWN position, dive the plane and pull out abruptly. Do this a few times. The centrifugal force helps open the wheel doors and lower the gear.

Emergency Operation of the Flaps

Use the hand pump first for flap extension because in some cases there may not be sufficient fluid in the main reservoir to extend both the gear and the flaps. You can lower the gear with the emergency extension system.

1. Coolant override switches and aileron boost OFF.

2. Extend the flaps ½ down by operating the auxiliary hand pump.

3. Lower the landing gear, then lower the flaps completely.

4. If you used the landing gear emergency extension system, raise the red handle to the UP position, and leave the by-pass valve in the CLOSED position. This maintains pressure on the landing gear cylinders, insuring that the landing gear downlocks remain properly engaged.

If one engine has failed in addition to the hydraulic system, remember, the airplane cannot maintain level flight on one engine with both landing gear and flaps down. Under such conditions, land with your flaps up.

ELECTRICAL FAILURE

Electrical failure may be indicated by a zero reading on the voltmeter and the ammeter, and by rapidly diminishing battery power. The first indication of a low battery is the failure of the propeller governors to hold the proper rpm.

An ammeter reading of over 50 while you are in flight indicates future electrical trouble. Land immediately.

If these conditions occur:

1. Set the propeller selector switches to FIXED PITCH.

2. Set the oil cooler flap switches to OFF.

3. Restrict the use of all lights and the radio.

4. If possible, turn the battery switch to OFF until you need electrical power.

If it is necessary to land with the propeller switches in MANUAL make the following settings to prevent overspeeding of the propellers in case you have to go around. Do this while you still have sufficient battery power to operate the propellers.

1. Altitude—not over 5000 feet above the airport.

2. Adjust the throttles and propeller selector switches to obtain 2600 rpm and 25″ Hg. at approximately 180 mph IAS in level flight.

EMERGENCY LANDINGS

The P-38's exceptional single engine ability will bring you home if one engine fails. If both engines fail or you run out of fuel, you have to decide whether to bail out or make a forced landing. There are many circumstances you must consider such as altitude, weather, and the type of terrain you are flying over. These factors have a great bearing on what you decide to do.

If you decide to make a forced landing, and can control the choice of a place to sit down, pick a spot near a road, phone line, small town or other settlement. This insures you immediate medical attention, or quick communication if medical aid is not on hand.

Prepare for the Landing

Unless you are lucky enough to find an airport under you, land with your wheels up. Don't attempt to land wheels down on anything other than a smooth hard surface and where you have plenty of room. Get rid of drop tanks. If you are carrying bombs, release them on SAFE.

Next, after you have selected your spot to land, unfasten your parachute harness so that after you land you can get out of the cockpit in a hurry. Make sure your shoulder harness and safety belt are on and locked. If you are wearing a Mae West, inflate it to take up some of the shock. Release the canopy and you are ready to land. Don't feather the propellers. Feathered propellers don't bend on impact. They dig into the ground, rupturing wing tanks and engine mounts, creating a fire hazard.

Landing the Airplane

Remember that with your wheels up the reduced drag increases the gliding distance of the airplane. Plan your approach so that you will land straight ahead and won't have to turn low to the ground. Land as nearly into the wind as possible. Lower flaps as necessary to get you into the place you want to land, but have full flaps before contact. This decreases your groundspeed and stalling speed. Cut the switches, mixture controls, and boost pumps to reduce fire hazard. Land in a normal attitude.

As soon as the plane comes to a stop, get out of the cockpit and away from the airplane. Fires have been known to start many minutes after a belly landing.

Belly Landings

If you come back to your field, lower the landing gear control handle, and find that the gear won't lower, that doesn't mean you have to make a wheels-up landing. Thoroughly and exhaustively try all methods of gear extension (**Refer to Hydraulic Failure**). Contact your squadron by radio and an experienced pilot will go through the entire procedure with you. As long as your fuel lasts you have time to work on getting the gear down.

When you are absolutely convinced that you can't get the gear down, inform the tower and prepare for a belly landing. The procedure is the same as outlined in **Emergency Landings** except that you have plenty of time and have a runway to land on.

DITCHING

The two major factors which necessitate a water landing are running out of fuel or losing both engines at an altitude too low to bail out. Learn the emergency radio procedure for your theater of operations. Your best chance for rescue lies in correct and speedy radio procedure before ditching.

The P-38 does not float. It is extremely important that you prepare to leave the airplane immediately after landing on the water.

As soon as you have decided to ditch the plane, unfasten your parachute harness, release the canopy, and push both side windows down. Be sure your safety belt and shoulder harness are on and locked.

Release drop tanks or bombs. If the water is very smooth, you can use the splashes the tanks or bombs make on the surface to judge your altitude.

Note wind and surface conditions and try to make your approach parallel to the swell and as near into the wind as possible. Don't lower your flaps. The retraction mechanism is such that when the flaps are down, surface pressure can't force them up. If you use flaps, they will act as diving vanes and force the nose under before complete loss of speed.

Make a flat approach. Keep your wheels up. Water landings with gear down are fatal.

Cut the mixture control and switches just before contact with the water.

After the plane has come to a rest, release the safety belt and jump out pulling the dinghy loose from the parachute. If possible, salvage the parachute. It will come in handy.

Inflate your Mae West and then the dinghy.

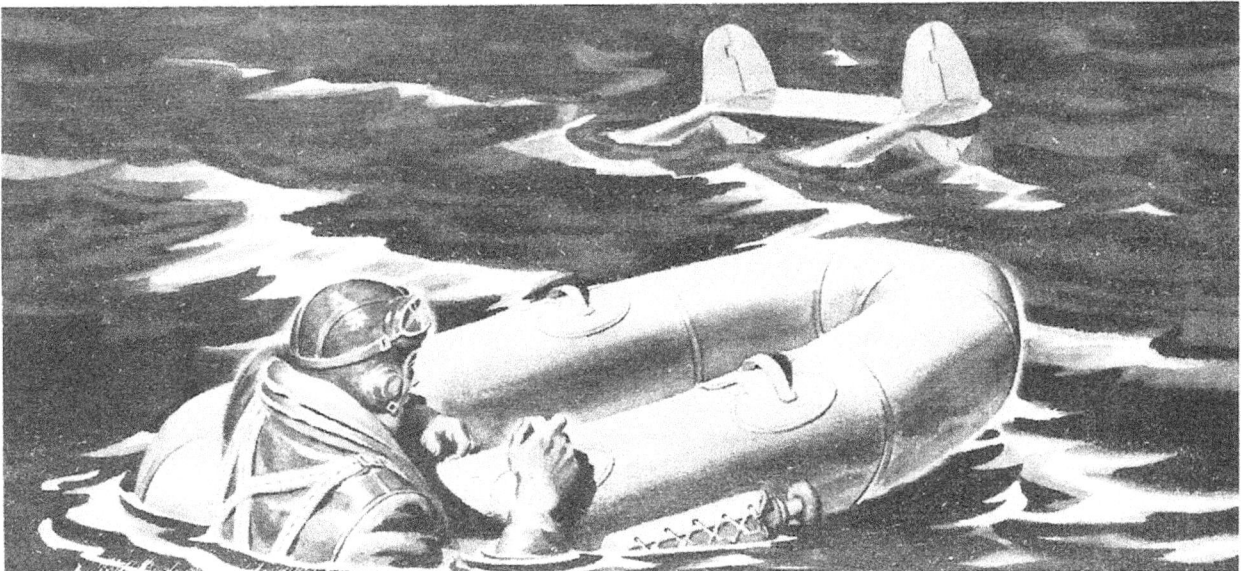

BAILOUT

Many stories have been circulated that you can't successfully bail out of the P-38. Rumor had it that you wouldn't have a chance of missing the horizontal stabilizer, and twin booms and rudders. Actual experience has disproven these stories. In spite of the hangar talk that crops up from time to time, **it is no more difficult to bail out of a P-38 than any present-day fighter.**

The method of leaving the plane is largely dependent on your altitude, attitude, and airspeed. The final decision on how to get out rests with you. Here are three recommended and accepted procedures for bailing out.

Over the trailing edge of the wing

1. Head towards an unpopulated area and disconnect oxygen tube and radio equipment.

2. Slow the plane down as much as possible.

3. Roll down the left window and release the canopy.

4. Release your safety belt and **slide** out **head first** off the trailing edge of the wing. **Never stand up or jump!**

YOU WILL CLEAR THE HORIZONTAL STABILIZER

Roll the plane over and drop out

1. Disconnect oxygen tube and radio equipment.

2. Roll elevator trim tab forward while holding plane level. (This will keep the nose of the plane up while you are on your back.)

3. Release the canopy and roll the plane over on its back.

4. Unhook your safety belt and drop out.

Unless you are very low to the ground, keep your hand off the ripcord when leaving the plane. If you hold the ripcord handle as you bail out, the slipstream jerks your arm and the chute opens before you are clear of the plane.

Sucked out at high speed

If your P-38 is out of control and traveling at a high airspeed, disconnect the oxygen tube and radio equipment, unhook your safety belt, and then release the canopy.

When the canopy is released, the vacuum created in the cockpit sucks you out of the seat and carries you clear of the plane.

If you feel conditions warrant leaving your plane and you have made up your mind to jump, decide which is the best way to get out, and then **go**.

ICING

If you anticipate icing conditions, or are in heavy rain, turn the pitot heat ON. Water or ice blocking the opening of the pitot tube can give you a false airspeed reading.

The formation of carburetor ice is unlikely in the P-38 because of the injection type carburetors and the heating effect of the turbo-superchargers. It is possible, however, for carburetor ice to form while you are flying at low power in icing conditions.

Remove carburetor ice by increasing power to supercharger range. Close the intercooler shutters (if installed) as far as possible without exceeding the maximum 45°C carburetor temperature.

If you want to add power and not increase your airspeed when flying in limited visibility or turbulence, lower partial flaps or the landing gear or both, as needed.

If icing conditions are present during a landing approach, move the throttles occasionally to prevent ice from freezing them in a closed position. With gear and flaps down, make approach under partial power.

You can remove ice from the windshield by turning the cockpit heat ON and directing the flexible heater tube to the desired point.

INDEX

AIRCRAFT AT WAR DVD SERIES

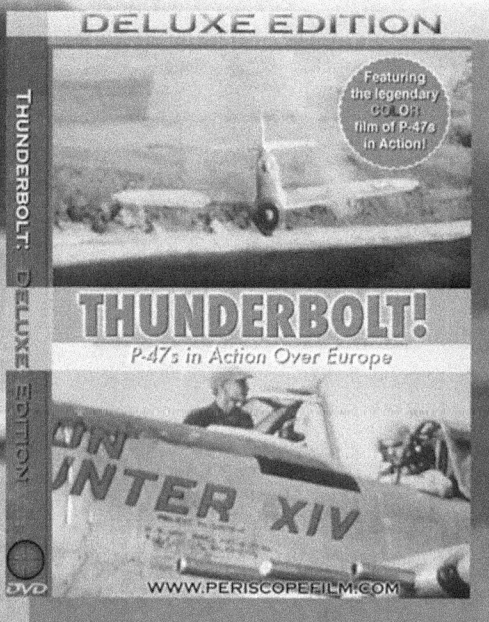

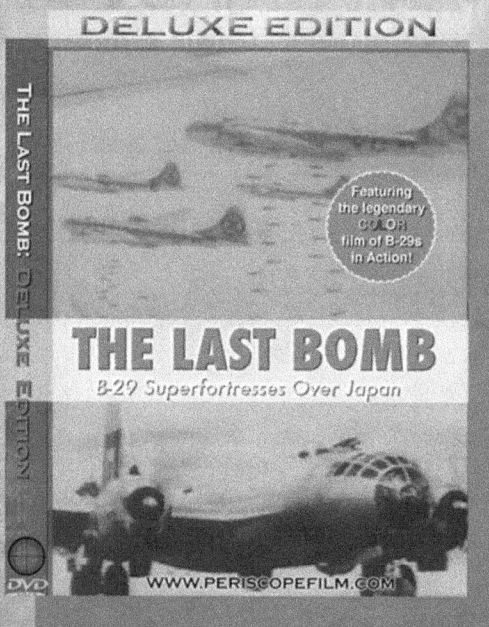

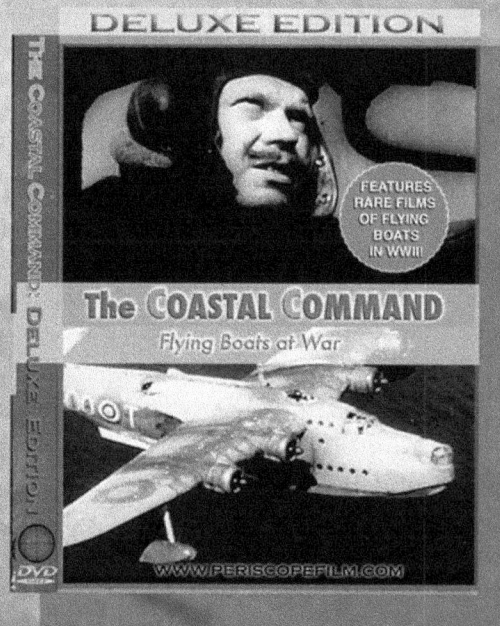

DELUXE EDITION

Featuring the legendary COLOR film of P-47s in Action!

THUNDERBOLT!
P-47s in Action Over Europe

XIV

WWW.PERISCOPEFILM.COM

DELUXE EDITION

Featuring the legendary COLOR film of B-29s in Action!

THE LAST BOMB
B-29 Superfortresses Over Japan

WWW.PERISCOPEFILM.COM

DELUXE EDITION

FEATURES RARE FILMS OF FLYING BOATS IN WWII!

The COASTAL COMMAND
Flying Boats at War

WWW.PERISCOPEFILM.COM

NOW AVAILABLE!

HUGHES XF-11
PILOT'S FLIGHT OPERATING
INSTRUCTIONS

HUGHES XF-11

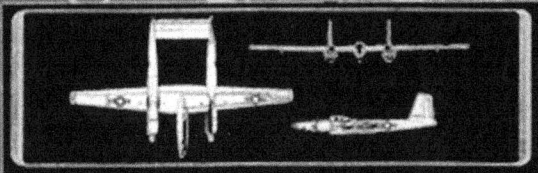

RESTRICTED

Originally Published by the U.S. Army Air Force
Reprinted by Periscope Film LLC

NOW AVAILABLE!

SPRUCE GOOSE

HUGHES FLYING BOAT MANUAL

RESTRICTED

**Originally Published by the War Department
Reprinted by Periscope Film LLC**

NOW AVAILABLE!

www.ingramcontent.com/pod-product-compliance
Lightning Source LLC
Chambersburg PA
CBHW081235090426
42738CB00016B/3315